# LANKIE TWANG

*A guide to the Lancashire dialect*

**Ron Freethy**

*with illustrations by Richard Scollins*

COUNTRYSIDE BOOKS
NEWBURY BERKSHIRE

First published 2002


COUNTRYSIDE BOOKS
3 Catherine Road
Newbury, Berkshire

To view our complete range of books,
please visit us at
www.countrysidebooks.co.uk

Designed by Peter Davies, Nautilus

ISBN 1 85306 770 9
Produced through MRM Associates Ltd., Reading
Printed by Woolnough Bookbinding Ltd., Irthlingborough

# CONTENTS

# FOREWORD

More than 20 years ago I wrote the foreword for Ron Freethy's book *Wakes Seaside Resorts.* His magic pen brought back many happy memories for me.

I am 'reet glad' to see that he has worked the spell again in 'Lankie Twang'. I love Lancashire and am proud of my native twang.

I was born in Morecambe in 1911 so in my lifetime I've seen huge changes. In my early days in Morecambe I remember day-trippers and folks coming for longer holidays pouring out of the station. It was possible not only to pick out a general Lankie twang but I could also identify miners from Wigan and cotton folk from East Lancashire whilst others were doing their best, but without much success, to be posh.

Lancashire humour is never far from the surface and we are never afraid to laugh at ourselves. I chuckled as I read about Lancashire humour whilst some of the dialect poems also brought a tear to my eye.

We've all enjoyed a drink of Vimto, sucked Uncle Joe's mint balls or a Fisherman's Friend but to me there's nowt like a good brew of tea especially if you share it with 'gradely Lankie Lads and Lasses'.

Enjoy the book and, if you get the chance, export it throughout the country – and especially into Yorkshire!

## A Lancashireman's Coat of Arms

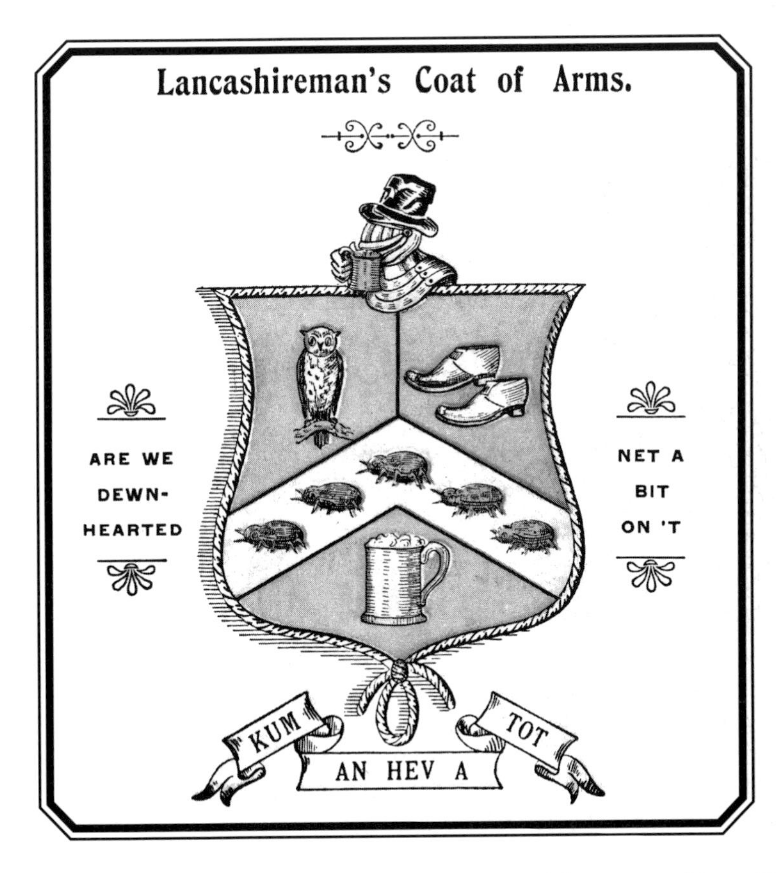


Any 'oft cumden' arriving in Lancashire can anticipate two things. Firstly there will be a warm welcome and a firm handshake. This will soon be followed, however, by a long session of leg pulling but the visitor will be expected to laugh and retaliate without the host taking offence. An uncle once greeted me with the phrase 'Tha's welcome lad, I've gitten nowt but tha's welcome to 'arf of it!'

One of my favourite poems was written by a Bolton man, Allan Clarke, who wrote under the name of Teddy Ashton:

*Sit thee dahn, draw up to t'fire*
*An' mek thesel at hoam*
*Here's a jolly good health*
*Here's luck and here's wealth*
*Whenever tha's passin this way*
*We'll allus bi glad*
*To see thee owld lad*
*Thar't as welcome as t'flowers i'May.*

*Teddy Ashton*

Hard work and firm handshakes typify Lancashire and this is personified in the tradition of the handloom weavers, who often 'warked themsels to de-ath'

**Work on a handloom**
Richard Rome Bealey (1828-1887)

*My piece is o' but woven eawt*
*My wark is welly done;*
*Aw've `treddled' at it day by day*
*Sin th' toime 'ut aw began.*

*Bu' nah it's ne'e to th'end o' th' week,*
*An' close to th' reckenin' day*
*Aw'll tek me piece upon mi back*
*An' yer what th' Master'll say*
*An' if Aw nobbot yer his voice*
*Pronownce my wark 'weel done'*
*Aw'll straight forget o' th' trouble past*
*I' th' pleasure 'ut's begun.*

# The Origins of Lankie Twang

I was born in a North Lancashire (now Cumbrian) village in 1936. My mother was a local but my father was Cornish. I grew up with a mixture of dialects which my schools, universities and teachers' training colleges did their best to eradicate.

Later I married a Burnley lass whose family had been long associated with the cotton trade and included mill managers, weavers, battery fillers, tacklers and twisters. I should point out that all these terms, including the last, were related to cotton. Other members of the family were associated with quarrying the local millstone grit, which was used in the setts (or stones) to construct the streets. There were also tram and bus drivers, a clippy (female bus conductor) and policemen. All knew and spoke fluent 'East Lancashire Twang'.

A series of elocution classes almost, but not quite, removed all traces of my beloved Lankie Twang. A teacher gave me one invaluable piece of advice: 'You need to retain the quality of your voice,' he said in his best clipped Oxbridge tones, 'and control your northern accent, but I would strongly advise you never to forget it – it is part of your heritage.'

I have had an abiding interest in Lankie Twang ever since and in my work as a teacher in God's own county and also during almost 30 years' experience in journalism, including work with the radio and television, I have learned to respect our dialect.

There are several areas of conflict which need to be understood. Firstly, a strong regional accent (wherever it is from) is not a sign of a lack of intelligence. Secondly, we should also remember that the Education Acts of 1870 and especially of 1944 brought correct spelling and pronunciation to the fore. Academics almost caused the death of regional speech and spelling. In the 18th and 19th centuries, dialect poets were too often regarded as 'dangerous eccentrics'.

## Where did Lankie Twang originate?

Without doubt our earliest words are of Celtic origin and academics are sure that Cymric, which was related to Welsh, Cornish and also to that spoken in

A Local Sken at
Nursery Rhymes
EEEK!
Tha 'as ter werk hard to get thi bait rahnd 'ere!
Little Miss Muffet

A Local Sken at
Nursery Rhymes
Weer do we stick this bit?
Gi it 'ere! I'll fettle it!
'E's fell on is 'ed!
I telt yon gobbin to gerrof yon wall!
Humpty Dumpty

Brittany, was in regular use up to the 8th century perhaps with some survival well into the 9th century.

Indeed Lancashire has more Celtic words in its speech than any other English county except Cumbria (including the area once known as Lancashire north of the sands) and Cornwall. I can remember my Cornish paternal and Lancastrian maternal grandparents using the same phrases. On my father's side were miners who moved to Cornwall when tin was declining and coal and iron ore were still in great demand in northern counties.

Cymric survived the Roman incursions but was first eroded and then all but obliterated by the Anglo-Saxons. What is now Lancashire was squeezed by a sort of pincer movement from the 7th century onwards by Anglo-Saxons from the south (the kingdom of Mercia) and the east and the north (the kingdom of Northumbria). Eventually the Celtic kingdom of Rheged, which embraced the area now constituting the Scottish borders to Cheshire, was smothered and 'Lankie Twang' had yet another language to absorb.

Next came invasions from Scandinavia, which brought more words originating in Norway and Denmark. My daughter-in-law is Danish and speaks our Queen's English more accurately than I do! When she speaks to our bilingual grandson in Danish, however, I am able to understand many words which those interested in our dialect still use frequently.

Initially then we must consider Lankie Twang as having a broad base of Celtic, Anglo-Saxon and Scandinavian – a unique combination.

'We are not a gormless lot – we is nobbut dif'rint'.

Perhaps the greatest influence upon our northern language comes from the Normans, who built castles and churches whilst their abbeys taught the scriptures and brought French into the hybrid. As an example of this take the dandelion, whose leaves are shaped like the teeth of a beast of prey. Get a Lancastrian to pronounce 'dent-de-lion' and you have our humble wayside flower.

Obviously each county has its unique form of speech, often deriving from various occupations. As many counties – including Cornwall and East Anglia – have remained largely rural, agricultural terms have flavoured the language. Lancashire has this element but during the 19th century the Industrial Revolution developed with remarkable speed, bringing with it words associated with cotton and coal, canal, road and railway construction, iron mining and smelting, plus other industries such as tanning and dyeing.

From the 19th century onwards there was an acute labour shortage and to meet Lancashire's needs workers arrived from many places, but especially from Ireland. During the 1930s and '40s workers came from European countries, especially Poland, which were threatened by Hitler's invasions. From the 1950s immigrants from the Indian sub-continent have added their quota to the existing Lankie Twang.

In the 1950s I overheard a conversation between a group of people in a Burnley pub.

'Thas nut reet – Tommy Lawton did laike soccer an' cricket at Brun-ly', said a Pole.

'Ah knas that's reet. Ah'm nay that gormless', said a Burnley lad in a cloth cap and with a Woodbine hanging from his lower lip.

'It meks no odds', grinned a Yorkshire chap, 'me sen I nahs that Lanishire cunna play cricket anyroads. Dost kna tha's still loosin' mishoneries from o'ert Pennines.'

Whilst I was compiling these notes I was travelling from Blackburn to Manchester by train and overheard two girls talking:

'Don't thi tell mi dad I'm co-orting. He'd bray me if he knew I'd copped on.'

'Nay he wudna belt thi wud 'e?'

'Nah, but 'e'd gah doolally.'

This could have been two milltown lasses talking in the 1930s – but it wasn't. It was two Pakistani girls travelling from East Lancashire to their university in Salford!

In the 1960s I was sad to think that regional accents were a thing of the past and were being destroyed by a combination of improved education plus radio, television and the ease and speed of modern transport. The e-mail and internet facilities haven't helped either. Not all is lost, however.

The BBC now accepts and celebrates regional accents, the old dialect poets are being re-read without folk 'fretting abaht spellin' and corict pronunciashun'. The future for Lankie Twang looks brighter than at any time since the 1920s and I hope that this present book, which includes a dickshunary section, will help.

What must not happen is for modern academic dialect writers to lay out artificial rules. We all speak Lankie Twang – let us continue to speak 'wot cums naturally to all on us'. Don't worry about spelling either – it cannot be written down in a manner to satisfy everyone – so don't try.

Although he was not a Lankie Lad, Stanley Holloway's monologues are probably among the most famous bits of Twang. To the Lancastrians, however, it was nobbut an attempt to 'try un' tell a tale of twang'. The Ramsbottoms and Albert, their young varmint of a son, have become world famous. The family's antics in trying to negotiate a Ferry Across the Mersey and the 'stick with its 'orse's 'ed 'andle', which caused Albert to get 'et' by Wallace the

A Local Sken at
Nursery Rhymes
Oo's laiking daft-buggers?
Little Jack Horner

*Freddie Trueman and Les Dawson seem prepared to debate the issue*

Blackpool Lion, still have not dated and are as comical as ever.

> *On the banks of the Mersey, over on Cheshire side*
> *Lies Runcorn that's best known to fame*
> *By Transporter Bridge as tak's folks over its stream*
> *Or else brings 'em back across same.*
>
> *In days before Transporter Bridge were put up*
> *A ferry boat lay in the slip,*
> *And old Ted the Boatman would row folks across*
> *At tuppence per person per trip.*

Stanley Holloway has gone, the old row-boat ferry has gone, the Transporter Bridge has gone but Lankie Twang and humour, thankfully, remain with us.

Before we begin to get to grips with a dickshunary, the last word must come

A Local Sken at
Nursery Rhymes
LANKIE TWANG
Weer the 'ells 'e orf ter nah?
What are thee moanin' at? Ahv gotta carry this great lumberin' bugger!
To 'ell wi' this fer a game 'o soljers!
The Grand Old Duke of York

*Stanley Holloway*

from the pen of Sam Fitton. He puts his finger most firmly on the Lankie pulse:

'Cum on lad th' knocker-up's bin.'

'I'b kubbid.'

'Eh Willie's cattahr does bother him in a mornin' sometimes.' (Heaw the heck dun they spell catarrh? Never mind!)

Nah then let's get on wi't Dickshionary – How do they spell it? – Never mind!

# DICKSHUNARY

## How to spake Lankie Twang

**Aboon** Above.

**Acker** A stammer.

**Ackersprit** When translated literally means a 'land sprout' and refers to root vegetables, especially the potato. When first introduced from North America the potato (related to the nightshade family) was at first expensive but thought to be an aphrodisiac and therefore worth the brass.

**Addicks Watter (Haddocks Water)**
A name for a very weak drink and could be applied to a poor beer or a brew of tea which looks as if it 'ad sin a ghost'. It resembled the water left over after fish had been boiled in it.

**Afterings** The last drop of milk given by a suckling cow. This was an important event when folk relied heavily on their cows' offerings.

**Agate** To start or get going. Still in regular use in the Burnley area, 'I were agate' meaning to move. It also relates to the Scandinavian word for a track or a gate.

**Agist** This is not a form of political correctness but a word indicating the letting out of pasture, particularly for the grazing of cattle. It is often shortened to *gist* or *gyste.*

**Arval cake** A funeral custom dating back to the Scandinavian invaders, especially relating to the Danes. It originated at the death of a king or noble person. Derives from *arf* meaning inheritance and *wol* meaning ale. Arfwol became Arval only in Lancashire and until very recently a funeral drink was called *arval-ale.* The men drank and often took the cakes home to be given to their families. The Wakes Feasts may have derived from this.

**Akint** Means 'the same as' and comes from the Scandinavian 'a kin to'.

**Ale-Can** A humorous term for a heavy drinker; still in use but it was once applied to John Collier, alias Tim Bobbin, one of the first dialect poets.

**Alley** A marble, and essential to what was a popular game in the county. Most were obtained from old bottles which had round glass stoppers. The well-off could afford coloured marbles, some of which were called 'blood alleys'. Cheap 'marbles' were made of baked clay and shattered on impact with 'proper' alleys.

**Asshole** This in Lancashire is not an expletive but a derivation of ash-hole. This was the space below the fire into which the ash fell.

**Awmas** Meaning All Souls Day, which is celebrated on November 2nd.

**Back-End** Generally means autumn but it also applies to the end of the week.

**Baggin** A packed lunch usually taken to work and especially relevant in the Fylde area.

**Bait** Another term used for a packed lunch taken at work not particularly restricted to the Lancashire mill towns. I heard a Burnley lad on his way to fish on the canal say to his mother, 'Can I tek two lots o' bait – one for misel' and t'other for t' fish wot's int' cut?'

**Bally Ann** Thought to be a polite way of saying that there was 'bugger all left in the larder'. The day before payday the housewife had to put all remaining scraps of food together to make a meal. At least the Bally Ann day kept the wolf from the door.

**Barm Cake** A large bread roll or plain teacake. Still in use and in East Lancashire butty shops you still hear orders of 'Bacon, egg an' sausage on white barm, luv' shouted across the shop. At one time 'barm' was a term meaning yeast.

**Barmpot** Yeast, also called barm, caused ale to froth. The good beer below the froth was full of substance but the froth was somewhat lacking. To call somebody a 'barmpot' meant that they had 'nowt worth having at the top of t' head'.

**Barmskin** Leather apron.

**Battin'** New cars are capable of 'battin' on at high speed'.

**Beck** Scandinavian term meaning a small watercourse. The further north you go in the county the more becks you find. To the south the word 'brook' is used, thus indicating Anglo-Saxon origins.

**Beestings** You can still purchase beestings, which are huge and very sweet custard cakes, in parts of the Fylde. Traditionally beestings was the first milk produced by a cow after calving. It was particularly rich and custard made from it was much in demand.

**Belter** Synonymous with 'blinder' and 'purler' and means excellent. The word is still used by radio reporters covering Lancashire football matches and also describing a lethal delivery during a cricket match.

**Besum** Used as a derogatory term for a bad tempered female. Also refers to a witch's broomstick.

**Billio** Used to express enthusiasm. I once overheard a camper, in 1950, describing his new paraffin stove: 'You nobbat have to leet it til it blows like billio.' The word is still in frequent use.

**Blackthorn** A girls' game played in the streets of mill towns before the days of traffic. The girls picked a leader, or 'blackthorn', who stood on one side of the street. The rest lined up on the other side and pretended to be a flock of geese. The 'geese' chanted:

*Blackthorn!*
*Buttermilk and Barleycorn*
*How many geese have you today?*
*More than you could catch and fly away!*

The group ran across the street and the blackthorn caught one, who was then 'out'. The game continued until only one was left and she then became the next blackthorn. 'T'childer were reet fit i' them days,' my Auntie Maggie told me.

**Boggart** To use the word 'ghost' would only be partially accurate. Boggart also refers to a mischievous spirit. They are here, there and everywhere, and are still alive and kicking today. 'Look at 'er – I popped the question and she were off at t' boggart', reported a rejected suitor in the 1940s.

**Brast** Used as a term of boredom but also means broken. The Brasts (spongy moss) of Pendle can be seen on the side of the hill, indicating a period many years ago when water burst out of the hill and flooded local villages.

**Brat** The 'childer' or bairns of Lancashire are not often called brats. This word is reserved for an apron, mostly those made of leather and used by cobblers, saddlers, blacksmiths and wheelwrights. For some reason the brat was also called a barmskin.

**Brew** Used to describe a hill (see **Brow**). Ha'penny brew, leading from the M6 motorway into Preston, dates from the early 19th century when there was a toll or turnpike road in this area. Also refers to a cup of tea and the first question a Lancastrian asks a visitor is, 'Do you fancy a brew?'

**Brid** A bird.

**Brobbing** Placing small twigs in the sand to mark the route for crossing Morecambe Bay.

**Brow** Meaning a steep hill, which caused problems during the days of the turnpikes when coaches were heavy for the horses to pull up the steep Lancashire inclines.

**Cant** Used to describe 'an old un' who is still active.

**Chat** Local name for very, very small potatoes. A delicacy until the 1950s was Chats and Dabs – a sort of mini fish and chip supper. A Dab is a very tiny flat fish which tastes very sweet.

**Chorley Pie** A traditional dish made with potato, onion, and minced meat topped with a sprinkling of cheese that was melted under a grill. Often served with pickled red cabbage.

**Chuck** Used, especially in the Fylde area, as a term of endearment. In other parts of the county 'luv' also applied but Lankie folk may have to watch themselves these days when political correctness is sometimes followed by litigation.

**Chunner** 'Mi mother in law is a mixed drink on 'er own – stout and bitter. 'Er nivver stops chunnerin'!' It means continually muttering. The comic Les Dawson often described his Lankie mother-in-law in perfect Lankie Twang.

**Cinder Tea** Children who were off-colour were dosed with this draught, which consisted of water into which was dropped a red hot cinder from the fire.

**Cinder Toffee** Still available in Lancashire's traditional sweet shops. It is a sort of honeycomb toffee but with a drop of added vinegar. It is bought in lumps which have to be broken and tastes like a Crunchie bar but without the chocolate.

**Clapbread** Another term for oat cakes, which were at one time the staple diet in the county. The name comes from the fact that the cake was clapped onto a hot stone prior to being beaten into shape. Still served in Lancashire with a slice of potted meat. It was then known as 'Stew an' 'ard.'

**Clod** A foolish person but also means to throw. I once asked a youngster how he had spent his weekend. 'Ah were wi' mi mates clodding bricks at bockles,' he replied, adding with pride, 'an' Ah wun.'

**Club** Used to describe sickness benefit but also refers to an insurance collector. Still in use today when an enquiry is made regarding a person's health – 'Are you still ont' club?'.

**Collock** Now only to be seen in museums, this is a wooden bucket with a long handle and used to carry milk in the absence of a yoke.

**Collop** 'Will tha tek a collop to go wi' thi eggs?', I was once asked by a farmer friend. He gave me the thickest slice of home-cured, fatty bacon that I have ever seen.

**Collop Monday** These days we accept Shrove (or Pancake) Tuesday as the start of Lent. In old Lancashire this period involved a three-day festival. This was Collop Monday, Pancake Tuesday and Ash Wednesday. On Collop Monday all the meat was eaten, with the last of the eggs being eaten up on the following day.

**Cop** There are several meanings of this word. It was the cone shaped pile of cotton yarn prior to being loaded onto spindles. It is also a small ridge of land such as is found at Cop Lane leading into Penwortham near Preston.

**Coppin-on Shop** A place where members of the opposite sex could meet.

**Crumpet** Also known as a pikelet this is a light, soft, yeast cake full of small holes on the top. Served toasted and soaked in butter.

**Dab** A small fish (see **Chat**) but also used to describe somebody skilled, i.e. 'She's a dab 'and at darnin.'

**Degg** Meaning to sprinkle; a watering can was until very recently called a deggin' can.

**Delve** The original meaning was to dig and only later did the concept of investigating a problem evolve.

**Dicky's Meadow** The origins are obscure, but this implies finding oneself in a difficult situation.

**Diddle-em Club** There was a tradition in the Lancashire mill towns of allocating a proportion of the wages into a savings club. The money accrued was paid along with the normal pay prior to going on holiday. All towns had a very small proportion of club officials who absconded with the cash, hence 'diddle-em club'.

**Dinner** In Lancashire the afternoon meal was referred to as dinner. In the evening tea was eaten. A man's proper dinner was often carried to the mill by his wife or one of his children. It was accepted that children would be allowed out of school to run to the mill carrying pies, a basin of peas or 'tatey 'ash'.

**Dolly-Varden** In the Manchester area this was a cart used to carry the contents of privies from the houses and down to the docks. The foul matter was then transferred to vessels to be transported to local fields where it was spread as manure. May

*Two Lancashire lasses examine a donkey stone. Nellie Corbis (left) and Benita Moore (right) are both sadly missed by 'Twangers'*

have originated from a character in Dickens' novel *Barnaby Rudge* who put on airs and graces. A Dolly-Varden cart was Lancashire's answer to those who needed a bit of a put down.

**Donkey Stone** An abrasive sandstone block with which ever-diligent housewives kept their front step in pristine condition. The name arose because the stone was wrapped in a package which carried the image of a donkey to signify hard work. Stones were often given by the Rag and Bone man in exchange for rags and old pots and pans. The stones were of white, brown and yellow, a sort of trinity for house-proud housewives.

**Doolally** A word for a person ''oo were wan sanwitch short ov a picnic' or 'nobbut ten pence in a shillin'. Such people were also described as 'duck eggs'.

**Dyke** Not only was this a damp ditch but also used to describe spying on courting couples.

**Eccles Cake** Still much in demand and baked using flaky pastry liberally mixed with currants, the best examples oozing butter. Crunchy sugar is sprinkled on the top. Modern day Lancastrians often have a pie and peas lunch with an Eccles cake for 'afters'.

**Eddish** A term for the growth of new grass immediately after cutting a crop of hay. When the weather is good a second valuable crop may be obtained.

**Edge** A steep slope leading up to a hill. Blackstone Edge near Littleborough and Standedge near Wigan are examples.

**Elder** A cow's udder and still considered a delicacy in some areas. The best offering of this dish is on Preston market. Considered by some to be superior to tripe and onions.

**Entry** A narrow passageway between buildings and meaning the same as ginnel and also 'rahnt backs'. Obviously popular places for courting couples when young ladies were not allowed to go very far without being chaperoned.

**Ewe Loaf** An alternative name for the Yule Log, which was the old-style Christmas cake. If you pronounce Yule in Lankie Twang you can see why the name ewe loaf came about.

**Faddy** One who is hard to please with regard to eating. The word 'kysty' is also used in this context. 'Yon lass is reet faddy – it's like trying to please a kysty moggy.'

**Fair** Strangely, the Lancashire word 'fair' actually means completely. 'I'm fair pooped' means that a person is totally shattered.

**Fangled** Fanciful. Newfangled ideas are to be taken with a pinch of salt.

**Fawse** Sly.

**Fettle** To mend. 'It's broak tha'll a' t' fettle it.' 'It's reet nah – yon's in fine fettle.'

**Fettler** A complimentary term for a friend. In the north of the county the word 'marra' may be used.

**Fey** Ugly or whimsical.

**Flags** Pavement.

**Flash** An expanse of water caused by hollows due to mining subsidence. Pennington Flash near Leigh is now a nature reserve and country park. Wigan Flashes is also a popular haunt of ornithologists.

**Flatrib** Derisory term for poor quality mild beer.

**Flea-pit** A run-down cinema but often with an exotic name such as Regal, Essoldo, Ritz, Odeon or Palace.

**Flit** Moving house. Those who arranged a proper flitting were 'reet foaks' but those who moved to escape problems were 'moonlight flitters'.

**Flummoxed** Flustered or confused.

**Fradging** Gossiping. 'There's nowt like a good fradging to blow t'cobwebs away.'

**Gabbing** Talking without stop and not usually making much sense.

**Galligoo** Mounds of toxic alkaline waste found in the St Helens to Liverpool area and around the Farnworth area of Bolton. In the latter area (called Moses Gate) a country park has been produced by landscaping the Galligoo.

**Gallivanting** Moving around having fun. My great-grandmother who was then 101 went missing and at midnight the police broke into her house (she still lived alone) to find it empty. Ten minutes later the irate old lady arrived home and accounted for her movements. 'Ah felt a' reet and so Ah went gallivantin' to Morecambe ont' train. Wot's that got to do wi' thee?'

*Peat cutting [see Moss Rooms]*

**Gammy** Injured. In the 1950s Barrow Rugby League International player Willie Horne was unfit to play against Wigan. The public address system announced "Orn's aht – he's dahn wi' a gammy knee.'

**Ganzie** A woollen pullover. This term is still in use and many Lankie lasses are still busy knitting ganzies.

**Gather** In the days before antibiotics even simple grazes went septic. Many sores 'gathered pus' and had to be treated, usually with uncomfortable kaolin poultices, which were put on the sore spot whilst still hot.

**Gawping** Staring in a manner which causes discomfort to those on the receiving end. 'What's ta gawping at?'

**Gip or Gippo** Very bad pain, usually in the stomach area. 'I'm reet poorly – mi bally is givin' me reet gip.'

**Gobbin** A person guaranteed to say or do something ridiculous. Tacklers' tales often show gobbins at work and at Oswaldtwistle near Accrington 'Gobbin Land' stories are still an important aspect of local literature.

**Goit** A channel leading water from a river or reservoir to a mill or other area.

**Gormless** A similar term to Gobbin. Gorm once meant to understand, so gormless is self-explanatory. In East Lancashire a large multi-headed gas lamp was once referred to as a gormless because it stood in the middle of the road and 'sed nowt'.

**Grinning Matches** In Cumbria this practice was known as Gurning. A contestant placed his head in a horse collar and pulled a face to impress the judges. Many northern comedians were exponents of this art, in particular Mr Vulgarity himself – Frank Randle. Les Dawson was also an excellent grinner who made us all laugh. In the early 19th century, Eccles Wakes Sports Day included grinning contests and an apple dumpling eating contest, also open to ladies.

**Gripes** A severe pain in the stomach area possibly caused by wind. Hence the childhood remedy of dosing with Nurse Harvey's Gripewater.

**Half-Timers** Prior to finally leaving school youngsters went half-time to school and half-time working in the mill.

**Hessian** A leather water bucket named after the shape of the boots worn by the Hessian Regiments. From the late 18th century a bucket of clean water cost more than ale. Water-carriers using their hessians made a goodly living but it was no job for weaklings.

**Hidin'** To slap hard. It may well derive from the tanning trade, which involved beating the hide to produce leather.

**Hippings (or Hoppings)** Stepping stones, which were crossing points of streams and rivers in the days prior to regular and reliable bridge construction.

**Hooter** Local term for a nose but also applied to the mill whistle, which summoned the workers earlier than they would have liked. The use of the hooter was suspended during the war in order for it not to be confused with air-raid sirens. There were occasions when hooters which were considered to be too loud were the subject of high profile court cases.

**Hush-Shops** Illicit drinking houses, many of which were around Manchester and Liverpool, and specialised in brewing poor quality gin.

**Hutch Up** Getting close together. 'Come on lass – hutch up!'

**Ill-Done-To** Not treated very well.

**Ill-Getten** Stealing or borrowing without permission.

**Ingun-Shire** England.

**Inkle-Weyver** 'Thick! He wer' as thick as a pair o' owd reawsty inkle-weyvers.' [Waugh, 1868.]

**Intack** An enclosed piece of ancient common land and synonymous with Intake.

**Irnin'** Cheese making. When a farmer started to make cheese he was said to have begun irnin'. An irnin-tub is the vessel in which the milk is placed in preparation for curdling. It derives from the Norse word *yrnan*, which means to coagulate.

**Jacob's Join** This is still enjoyed in my family especially over the period between Christmas and New Year and occasionally during picnics. It is difficult to know how Jacob got involved but the Join involved each person bringing an item to contribute to the feast. It is rather like a bottle party but involving food. The Join was particularly important when 'most foaks had next to nowt'. This was an important way of partying during the war with its associated food rationing.

**Jannock** A thick variant of an oat cake and thought to have been brought to the Bolton area by Flemish weavers perhaps as early as the 14th century. As well as items of diet they introduced textile techniques along with their religion as they escaped persecution.

**Jerry Building** Said to derive from Jerry Brothers, Builders and Contractors who built many 'second-rate houses' as the population of Liverpool increased.

**Jerry Shop** Illicit drinking establishment. Inferior beer was often served in these places.

**Jinny** A machine associated with the cotton industry. James Hargreaves invented a Spinning Jenny and may have named it after his wife, who was called Jenny.

**Jinny Greenteeth** Even as late as the 1950s my uncle scared me witless by telling me of a boggart called Jinny Greenteeth. She reared up from bogs and weedy ponds and 'swollered mucky lads 'ole'. The legend did serve the purpose of keeping inquisitive children away from dangerous stretches of water.

**Kale** There are several meanings. It could be a broth or a section of the crop rotation system.

| | |
|---|---|
| | 'Yo'st be wed when your kale (*cabbage)* comes.' |
| **Kales** | A game of nine pins (or skittles) thought to derive from an Old German game. |
| **Kaythur** | A cradle.<br>'I'll put th' chylt i' th' keyther an' set at yon wark.' [Bamford's *Life of a Radical*, 1840.]<br>'If theaw has no' bin rocked enough i' thy younger days it's time theaw'd a new kaythur made for thee.' [Ben Brierley, 1868.] |
| **Kayve** | To upset or turn over. We still use the phrase 'to cave in'. |
| **Keckle** | To giggle or to talk foolishly. |
| **Kecklety** | Unsteady and likely to fall over any minute.<br>'Aw'm as kecklety us o owd watter tub after o twelve munths' drought.' [John Scholes *Jaunt to see the Queen*, 1857.] |
| **Keck-meg** | A meddling woman. |
| **Keep** | Money given over for board and lodging.<br>'What does he get?' 'Nine shillin a week an' his keep; an noan bad wages noather.' |
| **Keepin' Company** | Courting and the length of this period kept many a Lancashire comic in material.<br>'Us been keepin' company fer 20 years,' said a lass, 'shud us get wed?' 'Aye,' replied the lad, 'but who'd 'ev us at our age?'<br>'How long does ta say they kept company?'<br>'Fer seven years; an' walked many a thasand mile, mon, while they were at it.' |
| **Kestlin** | A calf born prematurely. |
| **Kibble** | A stick. |
| **Kibbler** | Finding difficulty in walking. |
| **Kin-Cough** | Whooping cough – may derive from the fact that it spreads quickly by contact. |
| **Kitlin'** | A kitten.<br>'The brisk mouse may feed herself with crums until that green-eye'd kitling comes.' [Robert Herrick, *A Country Life*, 1648.) |
| **Knockus** | Knuckles.<br>'Hal o' Nabs had his knockus lapt in his barmskin.' [The works of John Collier, 1750.] |

| | |
|---|---|
| **Lace** | To beat with a leather thong or strap.<br>'Tha's gooin' t' reet way for a lacin'!' |
| **Ladelin' Can** | Vessel usually made of copper or enamel and used to transfer hot water from a boiler to the sink or into a dolly (or wash) tub. |
| **Laik or Laiking** | Old Scandinavian meaning to play.<br>Overheard on a train coming back from an East Lancashire football match: 'Licked agean – yon lot mun as weal stop laiking.' |
| **Laith(e)** | A barn or store house. |
| **Lant** | Stale urine used in the fulling of woollen cloth. It was a case of waste not want not because lant was kept in large receptacles in the garden for sale to the mills. |
| **Lea** | Old name for a scythe. |
| **Leather** | see **Lace**. |
| **Leather-Yed** | A blockhead.<br>'I can't say that I understand what it is you want exactly.'<br>'Well then,' was the reply, 'thou 'rt a leather yed.' |
| **Leavings** | Remnants left over, especially food such as offal. |
| **Ley** | Pasture or grass land, to distinguish it from that under cultivation. |
| **Lick** | To beat or surpass.<br>'Tha'll not lick that if tha tries for a week so tha might just as weel cave in.' |
| **Lilt** | To step lightly. |
| **Lime-Gal** | A pony used to carry lime. The 'gal' part relates to the fact that the best ponies for this job came from Galloway. |
| **Lish** | Active or nimble. |
| **Living Tally** | See **O'ert Brush**. |
| **Loane or Lonning** | A lane. As a youngster in North Lancashire one of my favourite walks was along Mucky Lonning to collect primroses. |
| **Lonk** | A Lancashire-bred sheep. There is still a Lonk fair held annually at Cliviger between Burnley and Todmorden. |
| **Lumber** | 'What's keepin' Bill till this time o' th' neet?' 'I hope he hasn't getten into lumber for 'e's 'ardly to be trusted on a market day – as owd as he is.' |

**Lurcher** A type of dog but also a person up to no good.

**Maddle** To confuse or irritate.

**Madlin'** A flighty or extravagant person.

**Mafflement** Hesitation.
'He're a fine, straight forrud mon, wi' no maffle abeawt him for o' his quare cranty ways.' [Waugh (1855) writing about Tim Bobbin's cottage.]

**Maiden or Clothes Maiden**
A clothes horse for drying clothes.
*'An iron't o' my clooas reet well*
*An Aw hanged 'em o' th' maiden to dry.*
[Waugh, *Lancashire Songs*, 'Come whoam to th' Childer an' Me.']

**Maiken** Used in North Lancashire for the yellow iris.

**Main Shore** The main sewer in a street.

**Marlock** A prank or a merry lark.
'He'd be makin' o' sooarts o' marlocks wi' th' bedclooas an' cheers an' drawers, tumbling 'em o' of a rook like an' owd goods-shop.'

**Mere** Lake such as Martin Mere near Southport, Marton Mere near Blackpool and, of course, Windermere and other meres in old North Lancashire (now Cumbria).

**Midden** (also **Muck Pit)**
Anything from a small backyard midden to a huge municipal dump of ash, rotting food and excrement. Each house had a midden in a backyard and the liquid run off was soaked up by the dumping of coal fire ashes. Middens were cleared out by men with shovels and a muck cart. 'E's gormless – dust na wot. He follered a muck cart an' thowt it were a weddin'.

**Mitch** To play truant or not being where you promised to be.

**Monkey Walking** Applied to young folk who strutted along regular routes in the hope of meeting a future partner.

**Moss Rooms** Specially allocated areas where local people were allowed to cut moorland peat for their fires.

**Naked Racing** Modern youth is accused of all sorts of lewd excesses but 'Notes and Queries' of Lancashire in the late 19th century show that our predecessors were not so moral either. Harland wrote: 'During 1824 I remember seeing at Whitworth two races at different periods. On one occasion two men ran on Whitworth Moor, with only a small cloth or belt around their loins. On the other occasion the runners were six in number, stark naked, with the distance being seven miles or seven times round the moor. There were hundreds, perhaps thousands of spectators including men and women and it did not appear to be anything out of the ordinary.'

It seemed that naked racing went on in Lancashire during the 1880s and they were prepared to dodge the police. On Rowley Moor (near Burnley) there was a riddle:

*'As I was going over Rooley Moor, Rooley Moor shaked,*
*I saw four and twenty men running stark nak'd;*
*The first was the last and the last was first.'*

What was it? The spokes of a wheel.

**Neb** — The point of a thing – the rim of a hat, the edge of a cake. 'Watch the neb on yon edge of t' shelf', i.e. your nose.

**Ninny** — A witless person.

**Noáger** — An augur.

**Noáger-hoyle** — A hole made by an augur. Also a game of marbles.

**Nook** — A corner.

**Nutters** — An affectionate name for the Bacup Coconut Dancers, a Morris Clog Dancing Troupe (all male) which blacks their faces and may well have originally been a Moorish group. They dance through the little town over Easter but they now also tour the world, spreading the fame of the county.

**O'ert Brush** — Couples having the courage to live together without getting married. Until the 1960s this was regarded as a mortal sin. Some irreligious couples placed a broom over the doorstep and jumped over the brush to signify that they did not care about convention.

**Off-side** — Feeling unwell.

**Oo-Dogs** — A rough game resembling hide and seek but played out of doors by teenage boys. It consisted of a 'man hunt'. The 'prey' was given a count of 20 to run away. The rest of the pack then howled (hence oo-dogs) and set off in pursuit. The end came when the 'prey' was buried beneath the pack.

**Ossie Cloggers** A traditional group with their dances choreographed to coincide with the space available in the old days between looms. These alleys with stone floors made a perfect 'sounding board' for the clogs.

**Pace Egg** A hard boiled egg painted or dyed and presented as an Easter offering. Still in evidence in the Preston area but at one time most schools and churches had well-organised competitions for the most attractive egg painting.
'Easter introduced a change. The slothful now demanded his pace egg (Paschal, old French for Easter) as a privileged Dole; the young of both sexes, on the afternoon of Easter Sunday amused themselves with eggs dyed by the yellow blossoms of the 'whin' gorse.' (Frank Hird, *Lancashire Stories* [1911].)
The conclusion of festivities involved rolling eggs towards each other to see which egg remained unbroken. The broken eggs formed part of the splendid picnic to mark the end of Lent.

**Paddy's Wigwam** An affectionate name for the Roman Catholic Cathedral in Liverpool.

**Pancake Tuesday** (see **Collop Monday**)
It was a tradition in Lancashire to leave the Christmas holly decorations up until Pancake Day, when the first offering was cooked using the dry leaves as a fuel.

**Parrock** An enclosure.

**Perry** To distribute money or other objects among a crowd.
'At the church door an idle crowd was always ready for the perry to contest for the scattered half-pence.'
Perrying still takes place in Chipping. The local children fasten up the church gates after a wedding and will not open them until the perries are thrown.

**Pikelet** See **Crumpet.**

**Pluck** The lungs of a farm animal. Pluck was boiled and fed to dogs.

**Poot** A young hen just about to begin laying.

**Poppin' Your Clogs** Meaning to die because 'nobody, however poor, ever popped [i.e. pawned] their clogs until they snuffed it'.

**Pop-Shop** Pawn shop.

*Fettling clogs for miners in 1939*

**Pot-Bo (Pot Ball)** A dumpling.

*What wofo' times are theese*
*Pot-baws are scant, and dear is seawl an' cheese.*

**Pouk** Small boil or a pimple.
'He does na need to mek a greyt to-do abeaht it; it's nobbut a bit of a pouk.'

**Purr** To kick and coming from the Celtic 'purr', to push or thrust. The Lancashire colliers had a 'sport' called 'purring' which involved 'kick boxing' using clogs which usually had sharpened irons called cokers on the toes and heels. Contests were fierce and serious injuries were commonplace.

**Queen** A prostitute in the 19th century. These days there is a different connotation.

**Querk** A moulding in joinery but also a term used for cheating.

**Quern** A handmill made from millstone grit. Quernmore (moor) in the Trough of Bowland was famous for the production of querns to grind corn.

**Quift** Drinking.

**Quiftin** Pot drinking cups.

**Quock** A term once used in the Fylde and meaning to be sick. Also means to travel some distance to work on the harvest fields.

**Rats' Nest** Untidy.

**Rawm** Wrestling or squirming, the latter applied to a child who will not sit still.
'Will 'im stop rawmin'.

**Reech** The smoke from house chimneys. When coal was the only form of heating the Lancashire towns had an atmosphere black with soot and the buildings thickly coated with muck. People who could not afford a sweep deliberately set fire to the chimney soot using old newspapers.

**Rec** Short for a recreation ground or playing field.

**Rent Dinner** After the tenants had paid their annual rent the master gave them a dinner. This tradition is not yet dead and a variant still exists at Downham in the Ribble Valley. This village is the setting for the television series 'Born and Bred'.

**Resurrection** The remains of a Sunday lunch warmed up on a Monday: 'A gradely wife wastes nowt.'

**Riggot** A furrow in a field.

**Ring Games** (see **Blackthorn**)

I remember watching a group of Burnley children in the 1950s playing in their schoolyard and the boys formed one ring in which they tried to trip up the rest until only one remained. Some wore boots and injuries were common. In the days of clogs the game would involve quite serious scrapes. The girls were obviously more gentle and their game involved melodic chanting:

*I'll buy a horse and steal a gig*
*And all the world shall have a jig*
*And I'd do all that ever I can*
*To push the business on*
*And I'll do all that ever I can*
*To push the business on*

*Waiting for a partner!*
*Waiting for a partner!*
*Go round the ring and choose one in*
*And kiss her when you let her in.*

When the lass was selected the lad was told:

*Now you are married you must obey*
*You must be true to all you say;*
*You must be kind, You must be good*
*And help your wife to chop the wood.*

This rhyme was quoted by Frank Hird in 1911 and was also a skipping rope rhyme, but with the pressures on the modern education system these harmless playground games (which were a spur to the memory) have gone. They are, however, part of our Lankie history and should not be forgotten.

**Rook** This does not refer to the bird but means a heap. 'Jus look at the clumsy clod – 'e's all of a rook.'

**Roop** A term used to describe a sore throat and a rough cough.

**Rops** Kidney.

**Rubbin' Rag** A person who has no influence. 'Ah don't need a rubbin' rag like thee – I'll ha' wards wee't screwdriver' (meaning the boss).

**Rubbin' Stone** see Donkey stone.

**Sad Cake** A very heavy cake made of soggy pastry rich in fat. Sometimes mixed using raisins or currants. Still popular today.

**Scavenger** A worker who emptied privies and middens. There is a story of a Manchester scavenger who made a good living selling false teeth, rings and other items found whilst sifting through the filth. Hence the word scavenging.

**Scouse or Lob Scouse**
Used to describe a typical resident of Liverpool; also lob-scouse was a tasty dish eaten by the poorer people. It consisted of a mixture of potatoes, onions and scraps of meat all stewed in water. Blind Scouse saved even more brass because in this the meat was omitted from the dish. My great-grandfather was a sailor and he always added ships' biscuits to his scouse. He also dipped wholemeal biscuits in his stew.

**Scratchin's** Pieces of chips, batter and fragments of fish usually hardened by cooking. Most fish and chip shops keep a few scratchin's for favourite customers and I love 'em.

**Seg** A hard callous produced on the heel of the hand as a result of using hard tools such as screwdrivers, hammers and even pens.

**Setts** Blocks of stone – usually millstone grit – quarried in

| | |
|---|---|
| | Lancashire. When cut into small pieces of regular shape the setts were used to construct the streets so typical of Lancashire towns. Many of these setts are still there but some have been covered over to produce a smoother surface. |
| **Sharra** | A coach or charabanc. 'There's nowt like a sharra trip tut' leets at Blackpool. Dost nah – Yates Lodge has gitten champagne on tap.' |
| **Shed** | A weaving area in a cotton mill. In Burnley's Turf Moor football ground the shed once meant a covered area for standing spectators. |
| **Side** | To clear or 'side' away the dishes. Also used as a derogatory term for those who thought they were posh. I once spoke to a man who met Thora Hird: 'A reet lady she were – not a bit o' side on 'er at all.' |
| **Sike or Syke** | Small stream; accounts for place names such as Harle Syke near Burnley. |
| **Sithers** | Scissors. |
| **Slack** | Small pieces of coal which did not burn very well. To keep a fire going during the night it was packed tight with slack and 'damped down' using cold tea. |
| **Slance** | To squint or to sken. |
| **Smoke Poke** | Early name for a mill chimney. |
| **Snap** | A packed meal – see **Bait** and also **Baggin**. |
| **Sneck** | A metal latch on a door. Also meaning a nose 'Look at 'er – 'er's gitten a sneck like a ferrit's!' |
| **Snigg** | To snatch; also a name for an eel. |
| **Sough** | A drain. |
| **Striking** | Crying. |
| **Swill** | Large basket made from bark and willow twigs. Used to carry coal, bricks, potatoes and other heavy material. |
| **Tackle** | Lancashire folk were a game bunch who would attempt any job. 'I'll tackle owt.' For many years the word 'tackle' has been used to describe a full set of male genitalia. |
| **Thronner** | A complimentary word for a person who is skilful with their hands. |

**Tick** To purchase goods on credit.

**Tickle-ish** A task difficult to accomplish.

**Tip** An untidy heap; also used to describe the spoil left over from mining or quarrying. Rubbish or refuse tips were also a feature of most towns – landfill sites are not new 'inventions'. Later the tips were landscaped: Barden playing fields in Burnley was once a tip and so was Otterspool Promenade on the banks of the Mersey at Liverpool.

**Trotter** A resident of Bolton. Pigs' trotters when boiled are still considered a delicacy in the town.

**Tup** To butt with the forehead. This obviously derives from the mode of conflict between male sheep.

**Uncle Joe** A name used to mean the pawnbroker. It was more polite to say, 'Ah'm short o' brass terday – I'll hae a quiet word wi Uncle Joe'. (See *Uncle Joe's Mint Balls* [chapter 4].)

**Victory V** Lozenges. They smell of chlorodine and were made in Nelson to a secret recipe. For many years Lancastrians believed that only Victory Vs were the 'reet sort of cough drops'.

**Waggin' Fat** Also known as Axle Grease. Was the name given to the first production runs of margarine. The term is still used today.

**Walking** Walk Mill near Cliviger relates to the days when fulling mills were created to produce woollen cloth free of dust and grit. The cloth had to be 'walked' through the process as it was treated with fullers' earth (which was expensive) or lant (urine), which was cheaper. The surname of Walker proves how common this process was.

**Walla** Bland tasting – like food without salt.

**Wamble** A sickly feeling often caused by being hungry.

**Warm** To strike hard. 'Nah then lad thee shut thi bone shoot or I'll warm thi backside' was often a father's response to a teenager who 'were feelin' 'is oats'.

**Welly** To give a good hiding. 'Up Welly' is also one of the neighbourhoods in Wigan.

**Weltering or Welting**
Pouring down with rain.

**Wet Nelly** A popular dish with the Merseyside poor. Stale cake was obtained from bakers and was soaked in hot syrup or treacle.

**Whisky Spinning** The hillsides of Lancashire were once dotted with illicit stills. On the Grane Road between Haslingden and Blackburn is a visitor centre containing a mid 19th century still which was confiscated by Customs and Excise officials. In the year 2000 there was a successful prosecution of a whisky spinner, so the practice is far from dead.

**Windmill Land** A name for the Fylde and coined by the Lancashire writer Allan Clarke (1863–1935).

**Wisket** A large flat basket woven from willow wands or reeds.

**Woods** The local name given to bowls. Crown green bowling is still one of the most popular pastimes in Lancashire. The Waterloo Hotel in Blackpool still hosts prestigious competitions, but indoor televised events have overtaken this location.

**Yammering** Muttering in distress. Also means lamenting.

**Yarber** One who gathers herbs.

**Yate** A gateway across a road or a fence. Between Roughlee and Thorneyholme in Pendle, Yate House stands at the crossroads to Newchurch and Barley. There is a Yate near Darwen and another at Penwortham.

**Yearth** A pronoun associated with earth. The use of the letter Y before a vowel is still common in Lancashire, also often taking the place of 'H'. Thus we have 'yead' instead of 'head'.

*My due reward, the right of which I deem*
*I yearned have ...*

Edmund Spenser, *The Faerie Queen.*
This 'y' in front of 'earned' would seem to prove Spenser's Lankie origins and his right to be considered as a dialect poet – perhaps the first.

**Yule Loaf** See **Ewe Loaf**.

# Lankie Laughter

## Ecksercise thi chuckle muscles

It is no accident that Lancashire has bred an impressive collection of comics. Some have managed to achieve national and occasionally international fame, although in some cases the Lankie Twang did not travel well. These comics plied their trade in the music halls where one script could be taken from town to town, so they could command a healthy salary on the strength of one good script per year. With the coming of television the demand on some comics to keep the flood of jokes coming almost on a weekly basis proved impossible.

*Ernie Wise, Thora Hird and Eric Morecambe in 1973*

The Lancashire list includes Charlie Chaplin, who was reputed to have enjoyed a dish of tripe in Blackburn market, Stan Laurel, George Formby (senior and junior), Gracie Fields, Tommy Handley of ITMA ('It's That Man Again') fame, Arthur Askey, Ted Ray, Frank Randle, Hylda Baker, Dorah Bryan, Jimmy Clitheroe, Thora Hird, Ken Platt, Jimmy Tarbuck, ventriloquist Keith Harris with Orville his green duck, and Ken Dodd. Doddy and Les Dawson were a couple who made the transition from traditional to modern humour but the best exponent was Eric Morecambe. All still drew on a rich heritage of Lankie Twang and the humour, which was woven in the mills and hacked out of the quarries and mines.

Many of the comics made jokes concerning drinking or avoiding drinking. The term 'teetotalism' is said to have originated in Preston. In the churchyard of St Peter's church is an epitaph, which reads:

> *'Beneath this stone are deposited the remains of Richard Turner, author of the word Teetotal and applied to abstinence from all intoxicating liquors, who departed this life on 27th day of October 1846, aged 56 years.'*

There was a rumour that Dickie occasionally fell into sin by sampling the evil brew and he may well have had sympathy with the author Andrew Tiraqueau, who fathered 20 children and wrote 20 books without the aid of booze.

*Here lies a man who drinking only water*
*Wrote twenty books, with each had son and daughter;*
*Had he but used the juice of generous vats*
*The world would scarce have held his books and brats.*

Comedians have adapted traditional Lancashire humour since Victorian times and visits to town centre pubs, especially following football matches, are still a source of humour.

A weaver was watching a Burnley football match at Turf Moor with his cap pulled firmly on his head. At the start of the match the weather was beautiful but suddenly it began to pour down. The weaver took off his cap and stuffed it in his pocket. 'What's tha tecking thi cap off fer int' rain?' his mate asked.

'If tha thinks I'm sittin' in mi 'ouse all neet in a wet cap tha's gitten another think cumin'!'

Lankie jokers often used vicars as their sounding boards. An old widow washerwoman of seventy decided to marry. A day or two after the wedding she met the vicar, who asked if she had decided to give up her washing.

'Eh dear o' me nowe,' she replied, 'I've noane gi'en up mi weshin'. I jus' fun' I couldn't wheel out the clothes by mysel' an' I'd to choose between wedding 'im or buyin' a donkey.'

Lancashire colliers had a tradition of dog racing, fighting and hunting. No doubt it gave them a welcome breath of fresh air as an escape from the pit. Lots of betting took place and a good dog could literally be worth its weight in gold. A vicar not happy with a collier because of the money he spent on his dog asked:

'What do you keep the dog on?'

'Beefsteaks an' mutton chops when I con afford em,' replied the collier.

'And what when you cannot afford them?' asked the vicar.

'Well then it 'as to live t' same as us.'

Dog fighting was a cruel but lucrative occupation in Lancashire, much of it taking place in the Liverpool area. In Harold Wilson's old parliamentary constituency there was a rhyme which noted that at:

*Huyton Huyton twa dogs fightin'*
*One's a black and one's a white un.*

Miners did not travel well and when they did visit London, perhaps when 'Wigan were up fer t' cup', southerners thought they were nobbut rustics.

In 1911 Frank Hird told the story of a miner who had to go to London to give evidence in a lawsuit. He was given a 'reet posh hotel' but scared other guests out of their skin by emerging into the lobby dressed only in his vest and long Johns.

'Wheer dost you wesh in this 'ole?' he asked indignantly.

'You will find water, basin and everything you require in your bedroom', replied the terrified girl on reception.

'Wheer did tha say?'

'On the wash hand-stand.'

'Does tha mean yon big jug?'

'Certainly.'

'Ah – that's wot I supped durint' neet.'

A Lancashire lad overheard a Welshman boasting about the height of Snowdon. 'Hasti never bin in Owdham?' he asked. The Welshman said he had not and the Lankie lad went on, 'Then tha's niver seen Platt's chimbly, at's so high tha canna see t' top for smook. When it gets out o' order, they ha' to send up a steeple-jack to fettle it; an' one day, a jack covered hissel' all o'er wi' indy-rubber, so he'd be o'reet if he fell. Well nah up he goes to fettle t' chimbly an' sure enough deawn he comes. An' what does ti think? Asted of gettin' kilt, he just started bouncin', and he kep' on bouncin' for days. At last they had to shoot 'im to stop 'im starvin' to de-ath.'

Lankie humour in the local pubs and factories has always been spontaneous but to the county's comics raising a laugh was a serious business. Take Arthur Twist for example. He was an acrobat who could pull funny faces and tell jokes. He changed his image by having all his teeth pulled out to enable him to make even funnier faces, and in 1934 he changed his name to Frank Randle. He chose Randle after reading a tin advertising a brand of mustard.

Randle's humour was vulgar in his time – his catch phrase was 'I've supped some stuff t'neet' and he made obscene noises with a horn. Wherever Frank appeared the local Watch Committee were always there on the first night. The result was inevitable – a visit to the local magistrates – but the comic was never totally banned from performing. Had this been done the locals would have rioted and the theatre bankrupted. Blackpool's Watch Committee gave Randle a fine and the comic responded by hiring an aircraft and 'bombing' the council offices with toilet rolls. 'I've dropped some stuff t'neet!' he wrote on each roll.

'I met a chap in a pub looking clemmed', quipped Frank, 'an' I exed him wot were up.' 'I's lonely,' he replied.

'I's reet sorry for thee, wot will tha sup?' asked Frank.

'I'll have a double whisky.'

This resulted in a rude noise from the horn and 'No wonder tha's bloody lonely' was the obvious but perfectly timed punch line!

Lankie humorists usually did not have just one talent – for example Ken Dodd and Gracie Fields had voices which would have made their fortunes in opera if they had the training and the inclination. In the late 1950s I was on the Island of Capri, on leave from the RAF, trying to buy a coffee when a voice said, 'Nay lad – they wain't be able to fathom thi accent.' They didn't, but Gracie Fields did and she even paid for the coffee!

I recently re-read a review of Gracie Fields' performance which appeared in the Blackpool Gazette:

> *... she was parodying Tosselli's 'Serenade' until its frail beauty hung in tatters about it. A lift of the eyebrow, a puckering of the lips, a sly, coy glance, an extravagant mischievous caricature of the pretentious prima donna. High notes she had reached beyond the compass of a*

*Gracie Fields giving an impromptu concert in 1937*

*Tacklers on their way out to a dance in their Sunday best*

> *common mortal, breaking one to laugh with a hoarse, guttural neigh, and another as the rope of beads round her neck was pulled tight and near to choking her. They chuckled and gurgled in the packed house. Then it came. 'Shurrup' commanded Gracie in her genuine Lankie Twang. It was a combination of talent and timing.*

Lankie folks have always looked 'on the bright side of life' and the music halls were always well supported. Such has been the optimism of the county that humour oozed (and still oozes) out of the factories. Cotton mills were a continual source of humour and the so-called Tacklers' Tales had a folklore all of their own. Tacklers, whose job was to repair looms, were also regarded as somewhat lazy and were said to 'sleep for England'.

A Lankie lad walked into a butcher's, pointed at a sheep's head and said, 'I'll have yon tackler.'

'That's not a tackler,' said the butcher.

'Ah nah that,' said the lad, 'but it will be if tha teks all't' brains aht.'

A tackler's wife was poorly in bed and the visiting doctor prescribed a powder. It was to be given to the woman, who was to have as much powder as would cover a sixpence. She seemed to get worse and the tackler was asked how much he had given her.

'It were reet,' he insisted, 'but I didn' 'ev a tanner so I gived 'er enough to cover six separate pennies.'

These tales were often passed on from father to son and some families moved from the mills to the music hall with little or no change in their act.

Frank Randle and George Formby senior followed this route as did Hylda Baker, whose father was a comic. Hylda was born in Farnworth near Bolton in 1908 and her act was one of the quick cut and thrust of a mill lass. She had a very tall, thin sidekick called Cynthia and the catch phrases included 'Look at 'er – she's not gormless – she knows you know!' Lankie folk above a certain age will remember that gormless was the name given to a large, multi-headed gas lamp.

It was not just cotton which brought prosperity to Lancashire – the coalfield was once one of the largest in Europe. Indeed in Wigan it was said that the town's wealth was based on three Cs: Coal, Cotton and the Canal, which transported both products.

Just like the tacklers who were the butt of humour, the colliers also took their fair share of 'stick'. A collier always came home black as coal after his shift, until brand new pithead baths and showers were installed. He still came home mucky despite the fact that his mate looked as clean as a pin. The wife tackled his mate, 'Dost kna' why my Ned's alus mucky when he 'as wun of them showers?' she asked.

'He alus uses 'em,' was the reply, 'but he wain't tek 'is cap off.'

Engineering has long been another of Lancashire's strengths. During the war a Lankie lad working on Rolls Royce aero engines was sent to America, where machines were being constructed under licence.

'We build ours to a tolerance of less than one thou,' said the American.

'Dost ta,' was the scornful reply. 'In our spot we meks 'em reet!'

You could also say something similar about Lankie humour. We still do it reet!

Even Lankie children have inherited the humour from their ancestors. Having taught children in the county for many years I have lots of experience in the appreciation of their harmless banter.

*Hylda Baker, with Cynthia, in a scene from her well-loved TV show*

*Tommy Handley*

A Cliviger child in the 1950s was listening to an explanation of the parable of the lost sheep. The lad expressed surprise that a shepherd would risk leaving 99 sheep in fox country to go in search of one sheep. 'It is because the shepherd loved all of his sheep,' said the teacher. The lad thought for a bit and then said, 'Nah 'e's not that daft – it were the ram wot wer lost!'

Not too long ago the relationship between the police and the public was also subject to friendly banter. The word 'Bobbie' derives from Robert Peel, the Bury lad who established the first police force and became prime minister in the 1840s. Jokes about the police were not then veneered with malice. Take the policeman in Bacup, for example. He found a dead horse in Henrietta Street but his spelling was not so good. He dragged the horse into Gas Street before writing his report.

A policeman found a miner lying drunk. He nudged the chap and said, 'What's tha bin suppin?'

'Whisky!'

'Were it neat?'

'Nah thi daft bugger, it were broad dayleet.'

The humour of miners was always straight to the point and brim full of banter. I am certain that this was a rich seam of laughs for Eric Morecambe. Eric was never the one with the 'short, fat, hairy legs' but the one with the glasses. Young Bartholomew (his stage name, Morecambe, derived from the resort) was so short-sighted that he could not serve in the war. He was, however, allowed to go down the mines and was one of the 'Bevin Boys'. Eric was sent to work at Moorfield Colliery at Altham, between Burnley and Blackburn. Even in his youth he was stage-struck and much of his later patter was picked up from the rough and ready humour of the miners. He wore his glasses 'down t' oil' and those who remember the lad make the point that he always made fun of the black rings round his eyes. These movements of his specs were later honed to perfection in his act with Yorkshireman Ernie Wise. I guess that Eric got lots of humour from winding up a Tyke!

I cannot watch a Morecambe and Wise show without having a laugh at the pit lad and his specs. In an interview he once described himself as 'a pit pony without its tail'.

'What did you do in the war daddy?' 'I was in the underground movement!' he replied, looking as serious as only Eric Morecambe could!

If Eric Morecambe's stage name was invented the same cannot be said for Jimmy Clitheroe, who was born in the town in 1922; but within months his family moved to Blacko, on the outskirts of Nelson. Jimmy never grew taller than 4 feet 3 inches but made a good living from his perpetual youth up until his death in 1973.

His first stage appearance was during a Tattie Pie Supper at Blacko Methodist Church, which still stands. The concert party he was with did a 'major tour' of the chapels around Oswaldtwistle and Accrington and his presence caught on. 'The Clitheroe Kid' later became one of the longest running radio series in history (1957–1972) and was later transferred to television under the title of 'That's my Boy'. His catch phrases were 'Oh flippin eck' and 'Some mothers do 'ave 'em'.

Jimmy Robinson Clitheroe was in his way a tough cookie and a successful businessman, owning race horses and betting shops. One of his 'off the cuff' remarks came in one of his shows:

'Mam – I don't care about homework.'

'Well we care and Grandad an' me want to see you in the first three.'

'Why – 'as grandad backed me each way?'

Tommy Handley was born in Liverpool in 1894. He was the son of a dairy farmer, which proves that the city was more rural than is the case today.

Apart from a wicked sense of humour he had an excellent singing voice and just prior to the First World War he was treading the boards as one of the cast in 'Maid of the Mountains'.

In 1917 Tommy joined the Royal Naval Air Service and there he honed his humour, which culminated in a music hall sketch called 'The Disorderly Room'. His humour appealed to all, including the Royal Family as well as his fellow Liverpudlians. Unlike many of his rivals Tommy Handley was a natural radio performer, probably because he was so well-read and a master of ad-lib.

Only a scouser could invent characters such as Mrs Mopp ('Can I do you now sir'), the Minister of Aggravation and Mysteries at the Office of Twerps, Funf the Spy ('I go, I come back'), the Civil Servant called Fuss Pot, and Ali-oop, who tried to sell saucy postcards on each programme.

In 1939 ITMA ('It's That Man Again') hit the airwaves and became an institution until Tommy died – probably from overwork – in 1948. Molly Weir, who played characters in ITMA, wrote that '... the idioms peculiar to various parts of Britain were a delight to him. That is why he loved to introduce in the programme such Liverpool words as 'scouse' and 'whacker', and I noticed that his eyes always shone with amusement in the scenes with Frisby Dyke, played by Derek Guyler, his fellow Liverpudlian. In those days the use of such words was very daring, and I think it gave him a pleasant sense of outrage to use such robust language within the sacred precincts of the spoken word.'

Programmes of old theatres and photographs of the period prove beyond doubt that Lankie Twang is always good for a laugh. Folks hereabouts are always ready to laugh at themselves and therefore feel that they can poke harmless fun at others. They don't even care if people poke fun at the food they eat.

It is no mere chance that has kept the name Mazawattee a guarantee of all "a lovely cup of tea" means. It is because Mazawattee remains now as always, unexcelled for the three essentials - Flavour - Fragrance and Economy

Mazawattee Tea

SOLD BY FAMILY GROCERS
IN SEALED PACKETS & TINS

# Food and Drink

## Get it dahn and sup it up

The traditional view of a Lankie lad or lass is still cloth caps, headscarves and Coronation Street. And of course they still eat stew and hard, tripe and onions, black puddings, tattie pie, beef and cowheel and pigs' trotters. Ask a Lancastrian these days and they will say that 'There's nowt like a good slab o' parkin.' I once heard a conversation between a market stall holder in Burnley and a young lady. She accepted her slab of parkin and said, 'Cun I ev a ticket for it – my old fella's just picken un up fer speeding through Padiham. Aw thowt I'd join 'im!'

But what is traditional Parkin? This recipe is taken from a wartime cookery book:

**Parkin**

Ingredients:

| | |
|---|---|
| 8 ozs flour | 1 teaspoonful ginger |
| 5 ozs oatmeal | 1 teaspoonful baking powder |
| 3 ozs sugar | 1 teaspoonful carbonate soda |
| 4 ozs lard | 1 pinch cream of tartar |
| 8 ozs black treacle | 1 teaspoonful vinegar |
| 5 tablespoonfuls milk | 1 pinch of salt |

*Method*

Melt treacle and lard to liquid and add to dry ingredients. Add milk and carbonate soda and lastly vinegar. Bake for three-quarters of an hour. Regulo 4.

The miners ate a lot of treacle because it was cheap. At one time miners' wives were said to have joined forces with weavers – they wove strands of treacle with oatmeal on their handlooms to produce parkin!

The saga continued as the rumour spread that treacle mines had been opened in several secret locations. The 'mines' at Sabden on the slopes of Pendle reopened in 1992 and have become a tourist attraction. This is a lovely spoof and the sales of real parkin and models of the miners are very reminiscent of Ken Dodd's Diddimen. They have also discovered a seam of black puddings, with a special team recruited to bend the puddings into shape. It is the steam emerging from the puddings which causes the frequent 'Mists Over Pendle'.

There were once treacle mines at Tockholes, near Blackburn, and when a miner was interviewed by an *Evening Telegraph* reporter in the 1950s he said, 'Dost tha kna, I's 'ed some jobs i' mi time. I were once mekin' paper chains aht o' fly papers but its got naht on mining treacle an' weyvin parkin.'

The whereabouts of the 'Tockus' treacle mines was a closely guarded secret but the 'Tockholes Treacle Mining Company' had a registered office and made plans to export 50 million tons per year. They even showed visitors the entrance but nobody was allowed to enter.

'Nahbody is privy to us secrets,' was the stern warning. The entrance did look surprisingly like an old toilet, but this was no doubt just a cunning disguise.

If Lancashire became famous for devising succulent menus from cheap food it is hardly surprising because 'brass were 'ard to find'. Many a miner or mill worker pawned his best suit on Wednesday to feed his family until pay day on Saturday when he retrieved his clobber for 't' footie match and t' pub at neet'.

*Treacle Mine notice*

*Treacle Mine entrance*

Some mill owners knew how to screw the last penny out of their workers and many set up their own mill shops, which sold groceries. Sometimes as part of their wages folk were given tallies which they were forced to spend in the master's establishment. Prices were high and the quality of food was low.

There were several attempts to fight these injustices but none was successful until the first Co-operative began to operate in Rochdale. There is now a museum on Toad Lane which celebrates the success of one of the most successful chain stores in history – local, national or international.

The paying of the 'divi' is still well remembered in Lancashire, almost from the day the Co-op was formed in 1844. From its inception folk who shopped at the Co-op could be sure that they would not be cheated with regard either to quality or quantity. Gradually the exports flowing out of the docks in Liverpool reduced the price of tea and nobody crosses the threshold of a Lancashire home without being asked, 'Dost ta went a brew?'

**A Sope o' Good Strong Tay**

By J.J. Baron (1856-1922)

*Some chaps are fond o' aleheawse nooks, an' pots o' frothy ale;*
*Some cling to pop an' some to books who glory in a tale.*
*But wimmin, whether weel or ill, owd, young or grave or gay,*
*Are fain to sup, go wheer they will, a sope o' good strong tay.*

From 1864 Abraham Altham had an important grocery business in East Lancashire. However, he soon specialised in selling tea and by the 1880s he was selling in excess of eight tons per week. There was even a song dedicated to the 'Prince of Tea', sung to the tune of 'Auld Lang Syne'.

*Its fame is known on every hand,*
*Where'er the traveller roams,*
*'Tis used and loved throughout the land,*
*In many thousand homes.*
*When gathered round the evening meal*
*With friends and family*
*What adds more to the joys we feel*
*Than drinking ALTHAM'S TEA?*

These days the supermarkets have closed relatively small neighbourhood grocers like Maypole and Altham's, but the name of the latter is still part of Lancashire's history. Altham's always hired a train to take their workers for a day out to Blackpool. Seeing a gap in the market, the firm laid on excursions for any traveller willing to pay during the Wakes weeks holidays. Altham's Travel Agents now transport Lancastrians all over the world to 'soak up t'sun and get rid o' their brass'.

East Lancashire folk can still remember visiting the UCP cafés and enjoying a good strong brew and a dish of tripe and onions. They would then tour the market and buy some black puddings, a slice or two of tripe and a string of onions. Housewives knew well a popular recipe for tripe and onions that is still a favourite in my house; or in the summer it would be raw tripe with lashings of vinegar. It was often the housewife's job to carry a jug to the nearest ale house and return with the foaming brew of beer to her man.

**Tripe and Onions**

*Ingredients*

½ lb honeycomb tripe
1 medium onion (finely chopped)
¼ pint water
Knob of butter
¼ pint milk
Seasoning

*Method*

Cut the tripe into inch size pieces. Put the tripe, onion and water into a saucepan and cook for several minutes until the tripe and onions are well cooked; there should be very little liquid left at this point. Add the butter, milk and seasoning and heat up again. It is now ready to serve. Delicious with hot crusty rolls.

Apart from suppin' ale and tay, Lancashire has a long tradition of temperance drinks and there are market stores which still sell sarsaparilla, other herbal drinks and health remedies.

One of Lancashire's most famous inventions is Vimto. John Noel Nichols was born in Blackburn in 1883, the son of a cotton agent, and was sent to the prestigious Queen Elizabeth's Grammar School. He worked first as a stockbroker's clerk and then in the service of a soap manufacturer.

In 1908 John went into business on his own account and described himself as a 'Wholesale Druggist and Herb Importer'. He bought in bulk and then broke the ingredients up into small packets which he then sold to herbalists' shops.

He also sold the ingredients for making up mineral waters for sale in temperance bars. One of his most popular concoctions was a non-alcoholic tonic which was said to provide those who drank it with 'Vim and Vigour'.

He kept this recipe to himself and rented a warehouse and office at 49 Granby Road, Manchester. In 1911, with profits booming, he moved to Chapel Street in Salford and in 1912 branded and sold his tonic under the name of Vimto.

The Nichols family have, thankfully, retained control of the product and its recipe. Vimto is quite rightly regarded as a Lancashire institution.

Another Lancashire institution protected by a secret formula is one of my favourite passions – Uncle Joe's Mint Balls, which have been made in Wigan since 1898.

*Now there's a place in Wigan you all should know*
*A busy little factory where things are all the go.*
*They don't make Jakes or Eccles Cakes or things to stick on walls*
*By Night and Day they work away at Uncle Joe's Mint Balls.*

*Uncle Joe's Mint Balls keep you all aglow*
*Give 'em to your granny and watch the beggar go.*
*Away with coughs and sniffles take a few in hand*
*Suck 'em and see and you'll agree,*
*They're the best in all the land.*

*Me Uncle Albert passed away from ale upon the brain,*
*The Doctors said that he was dead and would never walk again,*
*So they gave the corpse an Uncle Joe's and then stood back aghast,*
*Cos the corpse jumped up and ran t'pub and spent the insurance brass.*

This humorous song was written by Mike Harding, one of Lancashire's best 'Twangers' and the Hoghton Weavers Folk Group also twanged away in praise of Lankasher and Uncle Joe.

Uncle Joe's founder was William Santus, who was born in 1873. He did not have much brass because he was one of seven children born to a shot-firer in a coal mine. William was destined not 'to go down the mine with daddy' but set up as a stall holder at Wigan market and married Ellen Seddon. Although Ellen was a dressmaker by profession her family had a long history of splendid recipes for toffees. From 1898, when the couple were married, Uncle Joe's Mint Balls were produced first as a sideline and then and ever since as a major product selling throughout the world.

*We 'ad a pigeon it were bald and couldn't fly too fast*
*Never won places in the races, always came in last*
*Though it were bald, no feathers at all it won a race one day,*

*We give it an Uncle Joe's Mint Ball and it ran all t'bloody way.*

The actor Sir Ian McKellen was born in Burnley but spent his youth in Wigan. Uncle Joe's are beloved by the actor, who has handed out packets made in his native heath throughout the world. To the star of 'Lord of the Rings' there is nowt so magical as a good suck of Uncle Joe's.

This sweet was guaranteed to provide internal heating to colliers, weavers and those braving the elements such as chaps who stood on the open terraces of Rugby League grounds, where Wigan reigned supreme for so long. Uncle Joe's were the choice of real men.

As its staff numbers increased the company gave its workers the occasional party at which a famous Tattie Pie Supper and pickles were served.

*Thoose fancy tarts, so dear to hearts*
*O' ladies slim an' sly,*
*Are good maybe, but dear o' me!*
*They dunno satisfy;*

*There's some who nobbut seem to care*
*For prime ragouts o' goose an' hare,*
*They're welcome, if they'll nobbut spare*
*That good owd tato-pie.*

You may say that Lancashire Tattie Pie with its crisp crust is like any other hot pie, but there are differences; and the same applies to fish and chips, which had a few traditional twists to it. Many experts add a drop of beer to the batter.

When Fleetwood was one of the major fishing ports of the world it took tough men to brave the Arctic storms. Strong lads facing strong storms needed strong sweets and here we have the origin of Fisherman's Friend.

In 1865 Fleetwood was nobbut a smallish fishing port, but when James Lofthouse invented the herbal cough and cold cure syrup the town soon became busy exporting the mixture. There was a problem, however. The sea was often so rough that glass bottles frequently shattered. Then came the stroke of genius –

*Ian McKellen*

the liquid was soaked into a powder and pressed into a lozenge. These 'suck it and *sea* Friends' must surely still be one of Lankie's most successful exports, and the Lofthouse family are still in control. It has certainly been proved that the Fisherman's Friend does ease bronchial congestion.

When Lancastrians couldn't afford fish and mushy peas they ate chip butties, but their opinion of plain bread was hardly complimentary.

To a Lancastrian the idea of eating white bread 'wi' all on it taken aht' was an insult and in the Furness district the dockers sang as they ate their bait:

*Don't eat Loxham's bread*
*It makes you shit like lead,*
*Fart like thunder, no bloody wonder*
*Leave off Loxham's bread.*

Neither would you get folk hereabouts eating 'German black bread', but now, after a period of unpopularity, there is a growing appreciation of oat cakes eaten with cheese or potted meat. The latter, known as 'stew an' 'ard', was one of the staple diets almost since time began and was once served in pubs. Still for sale on local markets it is lovely grub indeed. My young grandson, who is half Danish, loves his stew and hard but he adds to it slices of polony. He insists on having grapes sprinkled on it – I now enjoy this concoction myself.

Oat cake was made by mixing oatmeal with salt and cold water and kneading it until it was flat and thin. This was then slapped on a hot stone or an iron plate with a fire beneath it and baked for about five minutes on each side.

'Hard' was a Lancashire variation which involved using soured buttermilk in place of water. This was hung up to 'mature', usually on a clothes maiden in the kitchen, and then eaten with potted meat known as 'stew'. This was made with shin of beef, which was steeped in salt water overnight and boiled until it thickened; the meat was then pressed in a basin. All this was typical Lankie food but it was even more authentic when a cow-heel or some tripe was added whilst the meat was boiling.

Hard working Lankie lads enjoyed their pint and missed their local pub when times were hard. Humour, however, was never far away.

'There were no bad ale in them days', an old weaver told me. 'It were supped too fast to go orf.' Youngsters supped Cod's Wallop. It took me many years to discover the meaning of this phrase. In Liverpool there was a mineral water company called Cod, hence Cod's Wallop for the kids. Each bottle had a glass alley stopper in the neck. When the bottle was smashed the alley was an excellent marble. Is all this a load of codswallop? I don't think so.

LOFTHOUSE'S
FISHERMAN'S FRIEND
NEVER UNDERESTIMATE
THE POWER OF A FISHERMAN'S FRIEND

# Dialect Poetry

## Can tha warble?

For many happy years I sat in front of classes of pupils, some very intelligent others not quite so, most of whom had what some described as strong Lancashire accents. I prefer to call it pure Lankie Twang.

I overheard one lad, who was brighter than the little lass who sat beside him. 'Er,' he growled 'if brains were gunpowder, she cud nert blow'er 'at off'.

Dialect for these wonderful folk was first heard at their mothers' knee and by contact with grandparents. It was not meant to be read or written but was just natural speech.

This twang still exists today but was even more in evidence in the 1870s, before the Education Acts made school compulsory and training colleges raised the standards of teachers.

It was also around this time that Lancashire dialect poets began to write humorous and sentimental rhymes. This was a new art form and these days has been honed to a fine but often a too academic art.

Having said that, I love the Lancashire dialect poems and the sentiments which they embrace. But who should we regard as the true father of the poets who still exist within the hallowed portals of the Lancashire Authors Association? We should all read these offerings, but above all we Lankie folk should listen to ourselves and others. Words and phrases which we take for granted very often mystify folk from other parts of the country. The Lancashire Sound Archive located in Clitheroe Castle is an ever flowing well of knowledge and the transcribed tape recordings of the late Benita Moore, a librarian, are an invaluable source.

Benita and I were once discussing the subject of Lankie Twang when she told me of an old lady who recalled:

'We had a reet grand te-ercher at our school and I wanted to give 'er a present. We had nowt so I could not afford owt. Well nah it so 'appened that me granny deed. I tuk some lilies from a vase int' front room wheer they were layin' 'er aht. I pinched a rose an' all and give it to 'er et school. I then said to 'er 'I'll bring thee some mo-er tomorrer – they's nut berryin' granny while Friday.'

If Benita was a modern mother of our dialect then the great granfer of 'em all was John Collier, who wrote under the name of Tim Bobbin.

John Collier was born in 1708 at Urmston, then a village between Manchester and Warrington, where his father was the curate and schoolmaster. John was destined to follow his father into the Church but when John senior became blind at the age of 46 somebody had to earn some brass and the lad became a weaver. Being a bright lad he found the work at the loom undemanding and after a few attempts he became an itinerant teacher. Eventually he was offered a permanent position as assistant to a Mr Pearson, the headmaster of a school at Milnrow, close to Rochdale.

When Pearson died suddenly John Collier was promoted to headmaster at the then princely sum of £20 per annum plus a schoolhouse. With his new-found independence John could develop his undoubted artistic talents – he played the piano, wrote poetry and became a very skilled artist.

It was said that he would 'paint owt', including altarpieces for churches and chapels, but his favourite commissions involved painting inn signs. By 1740 his reputation was assured and in 1744 he married Mary Clay, who was born just across the border in 'bandit country' – Yorkshire.

This so called rivalry between the white and the red rose is almost always humorous banter, as I discovered when I watched the comic Les Dawson interviewing fast bowler Freddie Truman. But I digress – John Collier was not so much a bit of an ale can as a lot of an ale can. Drink, however, did not blunt his abilities and he could always get beer money by producing inn signs. John also sold his poems from door to door using the pseudonym of Tim Bobbin. It is no accident that there is one pub called Tim Bobbin in Milnrow and another in Burnley – he must have travelled widely.

When John Collier died in 1786 he was 78 and left behind three sons and a daughter. He was certainly the first poet who deliberately penned dialect, with his most famous work being the long narrative called *'Tummus and Meary'*. He also compiled a book on '*Lankeshur Dialect*', which he gathered whilst travelling around the county.

## Lancashire Hob and the Quack Doctor

### A Tale

*A thrifty earl was tir'd of lonely cot,*
*Because the tooth-ache he so often got:*
*Six teeth were all he had to chew his food;*
*All gave him pain, but none could do him good.*
*Hob hearing Rochdale town did then contain*
*A famous Quack, that drew teeth without pain,*

*To him he flies, and, in a voice as loud*
*As Stentor's, thus bespoke him thro' the crowd:*
*'Ho-onist mon what munneh gi' ye t' drea*
*A tush ot pleagues me awmust neet on dea?'*
*'Six-pence' the Quack replies – Hob spoke again,*
*'On conneh do't me, thinkneh, beawt mich pein!'*
*'Ho, well enough', – Quoth Hob, 'Suppose I two,*
*Yoan do for neenpunce?' 'That I will not do.'*
*'Heaw mony then for twelvepunce winneh poo?'*
*'All that thou hast.' – Quoth Hob, 'They're just enoo.'*
*The Doctor took this for a country joke,*
*Till he saw Hob hard pressing thro' the folk,*
*And mount the Stage. – Quack now some mirth intends,*
*And slily for a pair of pincers sends;*
*Thinking he'd met one of those puny fools*
*Would run away from such inhuman tools*
*Hob takes the pincers, 'Vara weel,' said he,*
*If they'n fit yo, im shure they win fit me.'*
*Hob now aloft is seated in a chair.*
*With open mouth, in which the Quack did stare,*
*Who laughing, said, 'You have but six, I find,*
*And they're so loose, they'll wa with every wind.'*
*'Better for yo, yo know; do yo yer job.'*
*'Yes, yes, and quickly too,' my honest Hob;*
*'Hold up your head' – Oh – 'Here is one you see;*
*Come, hold again – here's two – would you have three?'*
*'I think ot Mon's a Foo; we bargint plene,*
*Poo these aw eawt, or set thoose in ogen.'*
*'If that be th' case, hold up again, my friend,*
*Come, open wide, and soon the work we'll end.'*
*Hob now extends his spacious jaws so wide,*
*There's room for pincers, and good light beside,*
*Cries Quack, 'Here's three, here's four', Hob bawls out,*
*'Oh,'*
*'Hold, hold,' says Quack, 'there something more to do:*
*Come, gape again; – here's five, here's six, and th'las*
*And now I'm sure thy tooth-ache pains are past.'*
*'That's reet,' quoth Hob, 'gi me meh teeth, on then.'*
*The Quack complies, and Hob his twelve-pence paid,*

HOB and the QUACK DOCTOR

*Then, in dismounting, to the mob thus said,*
*'They're arron foos ot six pence pein for one,*
*While for o shilling I ha six jobs done.*
*But still they're bigger foos that live e pein,*
*When good seawnd teeth may choance to come ogen.'*
*The Doctor stares – and hastily replies*
*'They come again! Not till the dead shall rise*
*One single tooth no more thy jaws shall boast,*
*I hold a crown thou ev'ry tooth hast lost.'*
*'Tis done' quoth Hob: and stakes a Charles's crown;*
*The Quack as nimbly throws five shillings down.*
*Hob takes up all and in a neighbour's hand*
*Secures the total; then makes his demand,*
*'Measter yo known eawr bet is, that I've lost*
*My teeth; and that I have not one to boast.'*
*The Quack replies 'tis true; and what by toat?'*
*'Why, see I've six neaw, eh meh owd scull-hat,*
*Ne sur, if yoan geaw wimmy whom, I'll shew*
*Yo e'ry tooth, ot e meh meawth did groo.'*
*The Quack ill vex'd he such a bite should meet,*
*Turn'd on his heel, while Hob said, 'Sur! Good neet.'*

Some feel that Tim Bobbin was not the best but there is no doubt that he was the first. The rest of these Lankie Warblers will be considered in alphabetical order. Obviously I have selected my favourites due to demands upon space. I have tried to address the balance in the bibliography but as the interest in Lankie Twang increases some omissions will become apparent.

## Ainsworth, William Harrison (1805-1882)

Although not strictly a dialect poet, Ainsworth was one of the best-selling of all Victorian novelists and he did include lots of dialect associated with his characters. His most famous work was *The Lancashire Witches – a Romance of Pendle*, which was published in 1848 and has been in print ever since. Nobody interested in the history of Lancashire and its speech can ignore this book, which has spawned a lucrative tourist industry based around Pendle. Born in Manchester and educated at its famous Grammar School, young Ainsworth trained as a solicitor but his literary talents eventually brought him riches and enabled him to study general literature, with a special interest in Lancashire's history. This is why he wrote so vividly about the county and why his characters are made to speak in authentic Lankie Twang. Ainsworth was also no mean naturalist and wrote poetry about the creatures he encountered as a boy. His verse about the carrion crow is just one example:

*The Carrion Crow is a sexton bold*
*He raketh the dead from off the mold;*
*He delveth the ground like a miser old*
*Stealthily hiding his store of gold*
*Caw! Caw!*

*The Carrion Crow hath a coat of black,*
*Silky and sleek, like a priest's to his back;*
*Like a lawyer he grubbeth – no matter which way –*
*The fouler the offal, the richer his prey.*
*Caw! Caw! The Carrion Crow*
*Dig! Dig! in the ground below.*

Ainsworth was always grammatically correct and made no attempt to use Lankie Twang except when quoting his characters, but he frequently used dialect words, as this poem clearly shows.

This is in complete contrast with Allan Clarke, who is better known by his pen name of Teddy Ashton.

## Ashton, Teddy (1863–1935)

Allan Clarke was without doubt one of the great dialect writers and he gathered his material on his bicycle rides, which were marathons by modern day standards. His first job was in the harsh environment of the cotton mills in Bolton but he was bright enough first to become a pupil teacher and then a successful journalist.

From 1893 onwards he produced a very popular *Lancashire Annual*, copies of which are still eagerly sought by collectors scouring secondhand shops.

Allan Clarke's earliest memories were of Blackpool and the Fylde, his classic book, *Windmill Land*, celebrating his love of the area. He eventually made his home on the Fylde and for many years I have collected his writings, strolled through the areas Teddy Ashton knew well and made notes detailing how things have changed over the last century.

Allan Clarke obviously had humour and this stands out like a beacon when he writes in Lankie Twang; but his words in so-called standard English are much more stilted and were therefore less successful.

Any young lad cooped up in a cotton mill would look forward to his Wakes seaside holiday and one of Ashton's best poems catches this feeling to perfection.

**A Gradely Prayer**

*Give us, Lord, a bit o' sun,*
*A bit o' wark, an' a bit o' fun.*
*Give us aw, in th' struggle an' splutter,*
*Eaur daily bread – an' a bit o' butter.*
*Give us health, eaur keep to make,*
*An' a bit to spare, for poor folk's sake;*
*Give us sense, for we're some of us duffers,*
*An' a heart to feel, for them that suffers.*

*Give us, too, a bit of a song,*
*An' a tale an' a book, to help us along;*
*An' give us eaur share, o' sorrow's lesson,*
*That we may prove, heaw grief's a blessin'.*

*Give us, Lord, a chance to be*
*Eaur gradely best, brave, wise, an' free;*
*Eaur gradely best, for eaursels an' others,*
*Till all men larn to live as brothers.*

## Axon, W.E.A. (1846-1913)

William Axon was a true 'Manchester mon' from birth to death. He was the Manchester deputy chief librarian before being appointed to the then prestigious post of literary reporter for the *Manchester Guardian*. This gave him contact with all the dialect poets and Lankie antiquarians of the day, about whom he published articles. No student of Lankie Twang can afford to be without copies of '*Axon's Annals*'.

## Bamford, Samuel (1788-1872)

Middleton-born, Sam Bamford was a somewhat 'nettly' character and one of the radicals who worried the establishment in Lancashire just after the French Revolution. Could the same thing happen here? In 1819 Sam was present at the Peterloo Massacre in which a huge crowd assembled to demand reform and more civic liberties. The militia charged the crowd on the site now occupied by the Midland Hotel and at least eleven protesters were hacked to death. Sam Bamford wrote what is now accepted as the best eye-witness account of the Peterloo Massacre. This is Sam's serious side, but in the course of a long life there were also happy moments and some of his dialect poetry is memorable.

**Tim Bobbin's Grave**

*An stoode beside Tim Bobbin's grave*
*'At looks o'er Ratchda' teawn.*
*An' th' owd lad woke within his yerth,*
*An' sed 'wheer arto' beawn?'*
*'Awm gooin' into th' Packer Street*
*As far as th' Gowden Bell*
*To taste o' Daniel Kesmus ale.'*
*Tim: 'I cud like a saup mysel.'*
*The greawnd it sturr'ed beneath my feet,*
*An' then I yerd a groan,*
*He shook the dust fro' off his skull*
*An' row't away the stone.*

## Brierley, Ben (1825-1896)

I am convinced that Ben, who began his early life as a handloom weaver, actually wove his own brand of dialect poetry. A man's loom was his lifeline and the huge, heavy instrument took a man to operate it. The machine was passed on from father to son and this was the origin of the word 'heirloom'. Ben, however, was a 'breet

lad' and he learned to read and write at Sunday school in his native Failsworth.

From 1863 Brierley was a journalist on the *Oldham Times* and was a founder member of an influential literary society specialising in Lankie twang.

**The Weaver of Wellbrook**

*Yo gentlemen o with yer hahnds an' yor parks,*
*You may gamble an' sport till ye dee;*
*But a quiet heawse nook, a good wife an' a book,*
*Is mooar to the likin's o'me-e*
*Wi mi pickers an' pins,*
*An' mi wellers to th' shins*
*Mi linderins, shuttle and yeald hook;*
*Mi treddles an' sticks,*
*Mi weight ropes an' bricks,*
*What a life! said the wayver o' Wellbrook.*

This rhyme reads like a handloom weaver's handbook if ever there was such a thing! Brierley is a common name in Lancashire and accounts for the confusion with another Lankie Rhymer – Thomas Brierley, who wrote some 'reet gradely stuff hissel'.

## Brierley, Thomas (1828–1909)

### In a Snug Little Nook

*In a snug little nook, by a rippling brook,*
*'Tis there that my true love dwells;*
*'Tis shaded by trees, and fann'd by the breeze,*
*And laden with witching spells.*
*There I recline 'neath the sweet woodbine,*
*And marlock* her raven hair,*
*I clasp her fingers where beauty lingers,*
*And we bask in the rosy air.*
*Then here's to the cot, the neat little cot,*
*Where my true love resides;*
*May it contain love's rosy chain,*
*And a fountain of pleasure-tides!*
*Marlock means to play with.

Thomas Brierley, living at Alkrington near Middleton, was also a weaver but he worked in silk. He also wrote 'The Silk Weavers Fust Bearin' – home.' These rhymes and others composed by the Lancashire Warblers of the period are invaluable chapters of social history at the time of the start of the Industrial Revolution. Their work has certainly not been taken seriously enough by many academic historians.

## Cronshaw, Joseph

In the 1880s Joseph Cronshaw was penning his verse in his own area, which he called *A Voice from Ancoats*. Ancoats was then an independent village on the outskirts of Manchester. This poem reflects upon how the area was then a green wonderland nestling close to cottages.

*There's a bonnie little dingle*
*Abeawt a mile fro' here,*
*Aw'm welly awlus theer;*
*Ther's a summat seems to draw me*
*Where Nature weaves her spell,*
*That's why Aw like to wander in*
*Yon bonnie little dell.*

Lancashire has a long history concerning the study of nature. Cotton operatives spent hours at their looms and colliers mined deep into the bowels of the earth. They all longed to head for the hills, often with their dogs. Some of their pastimes were cruel and included 'foxing, badgering, cock and dog feetin' but others were more gentle. Many naturalist and rambling clubs were founded from the 1870s onwards and members often wrote in dialect.

These artisan-naturalists used the railway network to its maximum efficiency and many developed their own mini-museums, often based in rooms above their local pub. This was the origin of the Bacup Naturalists, who still meet at their old pub, which is now an impressive museum and has not served ale for many years. In Whitworth there is a pub known as the *Railway and Naturalist*; at one time it was a perfect example of a meeting place of those who loved Lancashire and its wildlife. No one person loved his county more than Sam Fitton.

## Fitton, Sam (1868–1923)

Here is yet another writer of Lankie Twang who triumphed over adversity; despite ill health he had 'mo-er brain than brawn'. Born in Congleton, when he was nobbut ten young Sam moved first to Rochdale and then to Crompton. Although a sickly child he worked first as a doffer in a mill but was then promoted to piecer.

Sam had an artistic as well as a linguistic talent and his cartoons brought him fame. He was a sort of Lankie Hogarth but concentrating on the humour of the cotton mill. From the early 1900s he earned his crust from a unique form of journalism which involved his own artwork.

Sam Fitton chronicled serious problems but his infectious humour was never far from the surface. It was he who invented Tacklers Tales, which brought light relief to those who worked so hard, but he also focused on the humorous side of home life. I love his poem 'Eawr Sarah's Getten a Chap', which to me is Lancashire humour at its best.

### Eawr Sarah's Getten a Chap

*Eh, dear; there's bin some change in*
*Eawr heause this week or two;*
*Wheer once there used to be a din*
*It's like a Sunday Schoo';*
*We never feight for apple pie,*
*We very seldom frap;*
*An' what d'ye think's the reason why?*
*Eawr Sarah's getten a chap.*

*He comes o'courtin' every neet,*
*He fills eawr cat wi' dread;*
*He's sky-blue gaiters on his feet,*

*An' hair-oil on his yed;*
*He likes to swank abeawt an' strut*
*An' talk abeawt his 'biz';*
*He's 'summat in an office', but*
*I don't know what it is!*

*He's put eawr household in a whirl,*
*He's sich a howlin' swell;*
*I weesh he'd find another girl,*
*Or goo an' loose hissel;*
*Eawr parrot's gone an' cocked its toes,*
*Eawr roosters conno' flap;*
*We'er gooin daft an' o' becose*
*Eawr Sarah's getten a chap.*

## Gaskell, Elizabeth (1810–1865)

Best known as a novelist, Mrs Gaskell was a very formidable lady and although Knutsford is considered to be her first love she was, however, devoted to Manchester and Lancashire. In her works, especially 'North and South' and 'Mary Barton; a tale of Manchester Life', published in 1848, much of the dialect is in pure Lankie Twang. Elizabeth's husband was a Unitarian minister working in the poor district of Manchester, which provided lots of research material.

## Laycock, Samuel (1826–1893)

### Bowton's Yard

*At number one, i' Bowtons Yard mi granny keeps a skoo,*
*But hasn't mony scholars yet, hoo's only one or two;*
*They sen th'owd woman's rather cross – well, well it may be so;*
*Aw know hoo box'd me rarely once, an' pood mi ears an' o.*

*At number two lives widow Burns – hoo weshes cloas for folk,*
*Their Billy, that's her son, gets jobs at wheelin' coke.*
*They sen hoo coarts wi Sam o' Ned's as lives at number three;*
*It may be so, Aw canno tell, it matters not to me.*

*At number three, reet facin' th' pump Ned Grimshaw keeps a shop;*

*'Hes Eccles cakes, an gingerbread, an' treacle beer an' pop*
*'E sells oatcakes an' o' does Ned, he has boath soft an' 'ard*
*An' everybody buys off him 'at lives i' Bowton's yard.*

Sam Laycock stands towards the top of the list of Lankie Warblers despite the fact that he was born at Marsden near Huddersfield in Yorkshire. He lived most of his life in Lancashire. In common with Sam Fitton, Laycock was 'nut un elthy lad' but managed to keep working in the Fleetwood area, where he spent most of his adult life. He worked as a baker and then as a stationer, which must have been useful to a chap who spent all of his spare time 'scribblin'.

Sam Laycock produced a host of poems including *Twelve Lyrics* concerned with the cotton famine which took place in the 1860s and had a great influence on all who wrote about Lancashire during this period. He was a genius who managed to combine humour with the tragedy of life of that time. This is encapsulated in his poem 'Thee an' Me'.

*Tha'rt livin' at thi country seat,*
*Among o' th' gents an' nobs;*
*Tha's sarvant girls to cook thi' meat*
*And do thi bits o' jobs*
*Aw'm lodgin' here wi' Bridget Yates*
*At th' cot near th' Ceaw Lone Well.*
*Aw mend mi stockins, peel thi' potates*
*An' wesh mi' shirts misel.*

## Shakespeare, William (1564–1616)

It is now well documented that Shakespeare spent much of his adolescence as a player in the homes of the Catholic gentry of Lancashire. He then used the name of Shakeshaft, which was a very common name in Lancashire. His plays contain a great number of Lankie words. More and more 'serious historians' are accepting this and acknowledging the fact that the character of Malvolio was based on Sir William Farington of Worden Hall in Leyland – a 'real live' steward in the employ of Lord Derby of Lathom Hall, the site of which is now the base of Pilkington's (St Helens) Glass.

## Spenser, Edmund (c1552–1599)

Should we be serious in considering the Elizabethan poet and author of *The Faerie Queen* as the first of Lancashire's dialect poets? I think that this concept has a great deal to commend it.

Spenser spent some time living at Hurstwood near Burnley in a cottage that still stands. Young Edmund fell in love with Rose Dyneley but the Lankie lass did not return his affections. Many think that he wrote part of *The Shepheardes Calendar* at Hurstwood and back this up by spotting references which are pure local dialect.

It may also be that *The Faerie Queen* was dedicated not to Elizabeth the Virgin Queen but to Spenser's beloved Lancashire lass, Rose Dyneley.

## Waugh, Edwin (1817-1890)

Anyone who chronicles the poetry of traditional Lancashire will probably stand with Waugh by visiting his well above Rossendale. Is this the place to start a study of Lankie Twang? Probably not, although Edwin was certainly the man who marketed the product to perfection. Like Sam Laycock he chronicled the problems associated with the cotton famine with love and affection. His poem entitled 'Come Whoam to thi Childer an' Me' is among the most often quoted from when it was first published in the 1860s right up to the present day.

**Come Whoam to thi Childer an' Me**

*Aw've just mended th' fire wi' a cob;*
*Owd Swaddle has brought thi new shoon;*
*There's some nice bacon collops o' th' hob,*
*An' a quart o' ale-posset i' th' oon'*
*Aw've brought thi top cwot, does ta know,*
*For th' rain's comin' deawn very dree;*
*An' th' har'stone's as white as new snow;*
*Come whoam to thi childer an' me.*

*'God bless thee, my lass; Aw'll go whoam,*
*An' aw'll kiss thee an' th' childer o reawnd;*
*Thae knows, 'at wheerever Aw roam,*
*Aw'm fain to get back to th' owd greawnd;*
*Aw can do wi' a crack o'er a glass;*
*Aw can do wi' a bit ov a spree;*
*But Aw've no gradely comfort, my lass,*
*Except wi' yon childer an' thee.'*

Edwin was born the son of a shoemaker in Rochdale in 1817, and in his early years of grinding poverty he worked for a Rochdale bookseller named Thomas Holden from the age of twelve. He used this experience to become a more than competent writer and an avid reader to such an extent that in 1847 he became secretary of the Lancashire Public Schools' Association. This post meant a move to Manchester where young Edwin was able to mix with the aristocracy of the literary set.

To begin with he successfully wrote what is probably best described as normal English and in 1855 he published his first book, which was entitled *Sketches of Lancashire Life and Localities*, which set him some distance along the road to fame.

Waugh soon began to develop a social conscience. His writing in dialect is what we associate with him today and his 'Besom Ben' stories are classics of their type.

Far too many students of Lankie Twang seem to suggest that with the death of such masters as Laycock, Collier and Waugh the days of dialect poetry were at an end. History will prove the contrary and the dialect poets and poetesses are still alive and well. In the early 1970s local radio was established and the BBC appointed the late John Musgrove as the first supremo of what was then Radio Blackburn (now Radio Lancashire). John approached me and asked me to record a weekly programme about the history of Lancashire. I was at first reluctant because I pointed out that I was not a traditional dialect writer. Musgrove himself spoke the standard Queen's English as well as Lord Reith but when he set his mind to it "e were as broad Lankie as Sam Laycock ees sel".

John Musgrove helped me seek out the hidden history of Lancashire, which eventually resulted in a successful book on the subject (see bibliography) and he also encouraged dialect poets to record their work for the archives and posterity.

The words of Ada Gibson and Benita Moore have proved beyond doubt that our relatively modern 'lady larks' should play an active role in preserving our Lankie Twang. After all, we learn from the knee of our grandma about the facts and folklore of our beloved county. Do the Benita Moores of this world belong in the history of our great dialect poets and archivists? Of course they do!

**A Gradely Tatter Pie**

*When we were young,*
*Mealtimes were fun,*
*And here's the reason why.*
*Mi mother allus med the best*
*A gradely Tatter Pie.*
*Well now I've childer of mi own*
*And when to bake they try*
*Thi say there's nothin' thi like best*
*Than mum's gradely Tatter Pie.*

Bus Stop Scene 3
Wots ee ben suppin?
I'll bet thi its nut Vimto.
RS

# CHAPTER 6

# Folklore and Traditions

## Don't thi bi freetened

At one time naturally occurring events such as floods, thunder and lightning, hail or snow storms plus earth tremors were regarded as having occult origins.

When methane bubbled up out of Lancashire marshlands and occasionally burst into flickering flames these were regarded as will o' th' wisps or boggarts in a hurry. Jinny Greenteeth would be waiting to devour those who trespassed within these regions.

The feathers of barn owls roosting on the beams of old barns occasionally became impregnated with slivers of wood full of bacteria. As these organisms decayed they glowed, thus creating a phenomenon now known to scientists as bioluminescence. In former times a white owl glowing in the dark was regarded as a portent of death and the eerie screech the bird produced only added to the fear. Having witnessed this once and heard the screech of the owl and the explosion of sound as it left its roost I began to understand the superstition.

These superstitions were passed on from one generation to the next and it was only in the 19th century that literacy and learning developed to such a degree that logical explanations became more freely available. These explanations, however, were slow to become accepted and in some of the remote country areas the old beliefs are 'nut quite de-ad'.

Thus the idea of witches flying around on broomsticks and changing their shape

Weather Forecast.
(Storm expected).

from old crone to 'active' animals such as hares, deer and birds was also readily accepted. Domestic animals such as cats and dogs were also brim full of folklore and the term 'raining cats and dogs' may well take us back to these superstitious days. Take the beloved domestic moggy for example. If a cat tore at cushions or carpets with its claws it was a sign of a gale to follow. 'Thee tek a sken at yon cat – its raisin t'wind.'

People always looked closely at their cat and whilst researching this book so did I. During the gales of 2001 and 2002 my ginger Tom seemed intent upon scratching everybody and anything and had a very wild look in his eye.

I looked carefully when 'Ginge' washed. If he drew his paw all the way over his forehead did this mean that fine weather was on the way? Not recently, I have to say!

If he only washed the lower half of his face did this mean it was going to rain? I would say the answer was 'yes', but this wet period should not be blamed totally on my cat!

To play with and stroke a cat was a guarantee of improving health.

'Tha'll nut be clemmed if tha' laikes wi yer cat.'

There are still regular accounts of faithful dogs being in communication with the spirit world. Their howling when a person was sick was a sign of imminent death and the mutt refusing to leave the grave of its owner was thought to indicate that the soul had not yet departed.

We seem to have come full circle as many long-term hospital patients are now exposed to domestic pets as a form of therapy. This and lots of other examples tell us that we should carefully examine all local folklore before discarding its potential usefulness.

We have now ceased to believe in examining the entrails of animals in order to predict future events, but the behaviour of many living beasts besides cats and dogs was also once watched with great interest.

If you saw your first spring lamb with its face towards you then you were in for a spell of good luck. If the lamb turned its back on you, however, you had to watch out. I remember my father watching the 1940 crop of lambs prior to going off to war. 'I see more heads than bums,' he told me and I'm delighted to say that he returned home safe and sound.

Birds were always good for a generous helping of superstitions. Swallows, wrens and robins were always considered to be birds bringing good fortune and anyone who injured such a bird, either by accident or design, was courting trouble.

If swallows or martins began to build their nests about a house or barn then it was (and still is in countryside Lankie) said to be a sure sign of good luck to the occupier. 'The mo-er brids the mo-er fortune' was the saying. On the other hand, when these birds deserted a former site it was a sure sign of bad luck.

In the 1980s an aquaintance of mine bought a house and his first action was to knock down the old nests of martins and set up his ladders to paint the eaves. He fell off the ladder and broke his leg. 'Wat dist tha expec'?' growled an old farmer. 'T' martins wern't theer to keep an eye aht.'

Farmers also believed that if they killed a robin their cows' milk would be tainted with blood.

*A cock robin and a jenny wren*
*Are God Almighty's cock and hen*
*A spink (chaffinch) and a sparrow*
*Are the devil's bow and arrow.*

If a jackdaw landed on a windowsill of a sick room it was taken as a sign of imminent death, whereas the arrival of a white dove predicted the opposite. The old folks believed in hedging their bets because if the patient died the white dove was then said to be doing a good turn by carrying off another soul up to heaven!

Most counties had a rhyme about the number of magpies seen, the Lankie variant being:

*One for sorrow*
*Two for mirth (or joy)*
*Three for a wedding (or a girl)*
*Four for a birth (or a boy)*
*Five for rich*
*Six for poor*
*Seven for a witch (or a wedding made in heaven)*
*An' then I'll tell thi no moo-er*

All birds were watched carefully, especially during the breeding season. If anglers saw one bird they predicted cold weather, but if two of a kind were seen then it was more than likely to become warmer. The explanation was logical. In cold weather only one bird leaves the nest in search of food, the other remaining to keep the eggs or the young ones warm; but when both are out foraging the weather is likely to be warm enough for country walkers to be able to enjoy relatively clement weather.

The folklore associated with animals is rich but that connected with plants is even richer. In the days before the National Health Service and local pharmacies, the value of the village herbalist or wise woman was almost beyond price.

**Seven Simples**
(Anonymous poem dating at least to 1850)

*When Saturn did live, there lived no poor*
*The King and the beggar with roots did dine,*
*With lily, germander and sops in wine,*
*With sweetbriar*
*And strawberry wire*
*And columbine*

Sops in wine were clove pinks and the wire of the strawberry was the runner.

The following is a list of some plants found in Lancashire and uses to which they were put.

**Bog Asphodel** – Also known as yeller plant. Grows on wet moorlands. Its star-like yellow flowers and reddish stems were boiled in water by mill girls, the liquid being used as a hair bleach.

**Kecks** – The hollow stems of common hemlock were used by children as peashooters. This has been recorded by many eminent writers, including William Shakespeare, who spent some time as a very young actor and playwright in several Lancashire manors, including Hoghton Tower.

*'... Nothing teemes*
*But hateful docks, rough thistles, keksyses, burres*
*Losing both beauty and utilitie'*

('Henry V')

*'Thoose Wi' texts o' script yer i' ther meaths ot they*
*con shoot eawt as readily as paes eawt of a kek.'*

(Ben Brierley, Irkdale, 1868)

*'As boys, the name we gave to the stalks of the wild hemlock, which we used for pea-blowers, was kex. I am not aware that this is to be found in the Gothic with any similar meaning; but in the Welsh we have Cecys plants with hollow stalks, and in Cornish kegaz, which means hemlock; and I see no reason why this should not be regarded as a genuine British relic.'*

(Rev. W. Gaskell, 1854. Husband of the novelist Elizabeth Gaskell)

**Keddle Dock** – Ragwort and also the Common Dock.

> *'Last July has been remarkable for the great quantity of Keddledocks.'*

(MANCHESTER GUARDIAN, FEB 26 1877)

**Moss-Crop** – An accurate name for Cotton Grass, which in the early summer can be dominant on the Lancashire moorlands. The flower heads are white.

> *'Three neet-gowns o'th' best grey calico an' they were put aht int' yard, bleac'in' nearly a fortneet till they were as white as a moss crop.'*

(WAUGH –OWD BLANKET, 1867)

**Passion Dock** – Amphibious bistort, which is common in Lancashire. Once boiled into a pudding with suet, flour, onions and sometimes eggs. It was known as Easter Ledger pudding.

**Samfer** – Known as Glasswort, the Marsh Samphire grows in profusion on the muddy areas of the Lancashire coast. Still used as a pickle and served with roast beef but was also once used to provide one of the raw materials used in the manufacture of glass.

**Sweet Cecily** – Also known as the Roman Plant. Thrives in Lancashire, where the climate is wet. Its white flecked fern-like leaves, its white flowers and its black seeds all smell of aniseed. Used as an inhalant in a steam bath.

**Tansy** – An aromatic plant used as a flavouring. Tansy cakes were once eaten in the Bury district.

Witchcraft, or more likely the fear of witchcraft, persisted longer in Lancashire than in most counties, no doubt due to the Pendle Witch trial of 1612. Many words and artefacts survive from this period.

Hundreds and thousands of walking sticks, for example, were used to keep witches (and warlocks) at bay. The 'evil eye' was feared until well into the 19th century and the gentry stuck cake decorations to their walking sticks and then placed the artefact on their doorstep. The red dots of the confectionery were thought to scare witches and warlocks.

In the Trawden area witch bottles were hung around the neck as a talisman. Some were filled with urine, human hair and other materials in the hope that this would stop witches coming down chimneys or prevent the hags from changing themselves into animals.

**Witchwood** – Also thought to be a powerful charm, it was cut from a rowan tree with a 'domestic knife'. Once the rowan twig had been cut the cutter had to return home by a different route. It is worth remembering that the Norse runes relate to carving on rowan wood. In Lankie Twang 'rowan' soon becomes 'rune'.

Tolkein's *The Hobbit* and *The Lord of the Rings* were written when the author spent lots of time in East Lancashire around Stonyhurst school at Hurst Green. It is a total coincidence, but nevertheless of interest, that local lad Ian McKellen played the role of the wizard. I wonder if he sucked on an Uncle Joe's Mint Ball whilst waiting to go on set?

# Names and Places

## 'What's thi name, wheer is ta from and wheer is ta goin'?'

Our surnames are without doubt clues to the origins of a county's history.

In Lancashire, surnames relating to (small) towns, villages and even hamlets are common, for example Whalley, Dewhurst, Dutton, Worsley, Farnworth, Haworth, Dalton, Walmsley and Birtwistle. These all denote an ancestry often dating back many centuries.

Where are the Manchesters, Liverpools and Salfords? They are not so numerous, which suggests that the more common names probably arose prior to the 7th century when all settlements were small and people were named after their native heath. Another reason is that all our large towns and cities originated from groups of hamlets which gradually amalgamated. Our cities gained new names whilst the suburbs were often the more ancient hamlets.

As the Angles moved westwards from the Pennines they chose settlement sites above the rivers. These they called tuns, the place names Tunstall, Warburton (tun), Accrington, Hoghton and Broughton all reflecting this.

They first used words derived from Northumbrian Anglo-Saxon but, later, their being conquered by the Mercian Anglo-Saxons – led by Penda, their bloodthirsty Pagan king, who killed the Christian King Oswald (Oswaldtwistle) – brought about a new vocabulary and an amalgamation of two similar, but still distinct, dialects.

Midland English was typified by a change in emphasis. The Northumbrians used a hard 'c' or 'k' as in Lancaster, Castercliffe, Kirkham and Kirkoswald. The Mercians soften this to a 'ch' as in Chester, Manchester, Chadderton, and Church.

Most experts on the subject think that the river Ribble was first a territorial and later a language barrier between Northumbria and Mercia and later there was a second boundary, between the Anglo-Saxons and the Norsemen.

This is what makes Lankie Twang so unique and fascinating – it can change from one bank of a river to the next. Even some small streams were once boundaries and the best example is Ings Beck at Twiston. This tiny hamlet was on the border between Northumbria and Mercia.

The Anglo-Saxons were inclined to establish their settlements quickly; in contrast, the Norsemen first preferred to be more mobile and only when they felt secure did they establish permanent settlements.

The earliest large Viking settlements developed at York and Dublin, but with an important intermediate camp on the Isle of Man. The area now known as Lancashire was directly on the marching route between these settlements and Lankie Twang has been greatly influenced by these 9th and 10th century Viking movements. Toxteth and Croxteth were landing places (also known as staithes); Fishwick and Salwick were creeks where small boats could find shelter. 'Byrs' were farms, from which we derive the names Formby, Kirkby, West Derby, Roby and Crosby. Was Thingwall, close to the Mersey, an early example of a Tynwald or assembly area similar to the meeting place for the Manx parliament?

A look at a map of the Fylde also reveals a strong Scandinavian influence. The area was once known as Amounderness. Agmundr was the name of a Norseman and ness was a headland jutting out into the sea, as in Furness. There is still Wray, Arkholme and Arnside, along with the valleys of Hindburn and Roeburn. Signs of the Norse tradition of developing upland farms, operating during the summer and called 'saetrs', can also still be seen on maps. There is Summerseat between Ramsbottom and Bury, which is now a stop on the East Lancashire Steam Railway. The still attractive habitat is now a well-established nature reserve rich in grasses and associated flowers.

There is also plenty of evidence to show that the Norsemen and the Anglo-Saxons lived together in relative peace, as indicated by joint names. There is still Westby-with-Plumpton, Ribby-with-Wrea and Catforth-with-Cottam.

Many Anglo-Saxon settlements remained untouched, such as Kirkham, Lytham, Poulton, and Singleton. There were also Halton, Caton, Gressingham, Whittingham, Bentham and Warton.

The adoption of the name of the father can be seen throughout Britain but in old Lancashire typical Scandinavian names are incorporated. Examples are Ty-son, Gun-son, Daw-son and Ben-son. The last name is still very common in the Flookborough area, where the Bensons have long been among the folk who earn their living from shrimping, cockling and fishing.

Only in modern times when people became ever more literate did the actual signing of Christian and surnames become important. Also precise spelling began to assume significance. Prior to this Lankie names were often long and read more like a studbook than a signature on a cheque or an entry in a register. For instance 'Bill o' Jacks up't brew and dahn't ginnel' was a better form of identification than having to locate one of several Bill Joneses or William Browns. It is almost as if we were to sign our name and then include our address, although this would be even more confusing as we tend to flit a lot. Imagine trying to sign a credit card which included details of where you lived and how to get there!

Many dialect writers of a later age chose to write under pseudonyms. The Rochdale writer William Baron wrote amusing poems around 1910 under the name of Bill o' Jacks. One of his best was called *Raisin' the Wind:*

*Owd Jonas Lee wur ceawer'd i' th' nook,*
*His ees were red wi' drinkin';*
*He filled his pipe to hev a smook*
*An' then begun a thinkin'.*
*'Aw'd swig a pint off neaw,' he sed*
*'An quick too if aw hed it;*
*But t' thowt ont' nobbut meks me long*
*For Aw've noather brass nor credit.'*

Brewers made brass and many made their fortunes. This also applied to millers, who developed a powerful local monopoly. Miller is a common surname everywhere but Lancashire Millers had a reputation for striking a hard bargain. 'What's up wi' thee?' asked a Lancashire farmer. 'Dost tha' not kna' that coin is med to gah rahnd?'

'Aye I knas that as well as thee, but they were also med brass flat for 'em to pile up.'

Throughout this book we have been celebrating our Lankie Twang and its illustrious history. Is there any future for our northern language? Of course there is, and just as humour will never die, so it is certain that our beloved dialect will survive.

Lankie Twang also needs its share of nostalgia and I think that Benita Moore should have the last word:

*Most people think of Lancashire*
*As County of the Poor,*
*They do not see the green green hills*
*And purpled heathered moor*
*Yet I see only beauty*
*Not the dark Satanic mill*
*When the sky is flushed with sunrise*
*And the snow's on Pendle Hill.*

The Battle of Hastings – AD 1066

The Battle of Agincourt — 1415

Richard III at Bosworth – 1485

Nelson at Trafalgar — 1805

The Charge of the Light Brigade – 1854

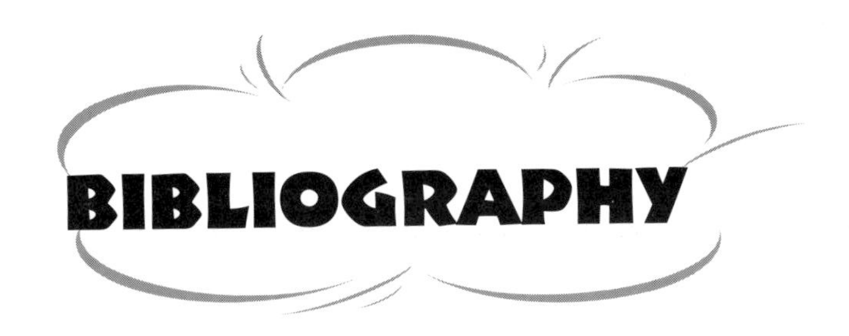


## A Lancashire Bibliography


| | |
|---|---|
| Ainsworth, W H | *The Lancashire Witches* (Manchester 1870) |
| Axon, W E A | *A Lancashire Treasury* (Manchester 1880) |
| Banks, Mrs G Linnaeus | *The Manchester Man* (Manchester 1896) |
| Bobbin, Tim | *The Complete Works* (John Heywood 1862) |
| Brierley, Ben | *Ab-o'th-Yate: Sketches and Short Stories* (Clegg 1896) |
| Brighouse, Harold | *Hobson's Choice* (the novel) (Northern Classic Reprints 1996) |
| Clarke, A | *Lancashire Annual* (Allan Clarke from 1893–1930) |
| Clarke, A | *Windmill Land* (Manchester 1905) |
| Collins, H C | *The Roof of Lancashire* (Dent 1950) |
| Collins, H C | *Lancashire Plain and Seaboard* (Dent 1953) |
| Dobbs, L | *Songs of a Lancashire Warbler* (Printwise 1992) |
| Dutton, D | *Dave Dutton's Completely Lanky* (Dutton 1982) |
| Eyre, Kathleen | *Sand-Grown, The Lytham St Annes Story* (1968) |
| Eyre, Kathleen | *Bygone Blackpool* (Hendon 1971) |
| Fitton, Sam | *Gradely Lancashire* (Whittaker 1929) |
| Fowler, A and Wyke, T | *Mirth in the Mill: the Gradely World of Sam Fitton* (Oldham Leisure Services 1995) |
| Freethy, Marlene | *Grandma's Country Kitchen* (Countryside Publications 1987) |
| Freethy, Ron | *Wakes Seaside Resorts* (Faust 1986) |
| Freethy, Ron | *Hidden Lancashire* (Countryside Books 1997) |
| Freethy, Ron | *Lancashire Privies* (Countryside Books 1998) |
| Graham, F | *Old Inns and Taverns of Lancashire* (Frank Graham 1988) |
| Heyes, C (Ed) | *The Best of Old Lancashire in Poetry and Verse* (Printwise 1992) |

| | |
|---|---|
| Harland, J and Wilkinson, T | *Lancashire Legends, Traditions, Pageants and Sports* (Routledge 1873) |
| Hird, F | *Lancashire Stories* (Hird 1911) |
| Houghton, Stanley | *Hindle Wakes* (Play produced in 1912) |
| Lofthouse, J | *Countryside North* (Hale 1965) |
| Lofthouse, J | *Portrait of Lancashire* (Hale 1967) |
| Mather, G | *Tacklers' Tales* (Palatine Publishing 1993) |
| Mitchell, W R | *Lancashire Mill Town Traditions* (Dalesman 1977) |
| Moore, Benita | *Lancashire Mixture* (Owl Books 1993) |
| Neill, R | *Mist Over Pendle* (Hutchinson 1951) |
| Neill, R | *The Mills of Colne* (Hutchinson 1958) |
| Nichols, S | *The Story of Vimto* (Carnegie 1994) |
| Richards, J | *Stars in their Eyes: Lancashire stars of stage, screen and radio* (Lancashire County Books 1994) |
| Roby, John | *Traditions of Lancashire* (2 vols. 1829 & 1831 published in Manchester) |
| Waugh, E | *Lancashire Sketches* (Manchester 1868) |
| Waugh, E | *Factory Folk during the Cotton Famine* (Heywood, Manchester 1881) |
| Weir, Molly | *Stepping into the Spotlight – the ITMA Years* (Hutchinson 1975) |
| Whittaker, G (Ed) | *A Lancashire Garland (Whittaker 1936)* |
| Wright, P | *Lancashire Dialect* (Dalesman 1976) |
| Yates, M (Ed) | *A Lancashire Anthology* (University of Liverpool Press 1923) |